PERSUASIVE SPEAKING

SCOTT, FORESMAN'S 〜〜〜 COLLEGE SPEECH SERIES

THEODORE CLEVENGER, JR.
GENERAL EDITOR
UNIVERSITY OF TEXAS

THOMAS M. SCHEIDEL

UNIVERSITY OF ILLINOIS

PERSUASIVE SPEAKING

DOUGLAS EHNINGER
CONSULTING EDITOR IN SPEECH
STATE UNIVERSITY OF IOWA

SCOTT, FORESMAN AND COMPANY

Dedicated to
Amanda J. Anderson
Howard W. Runkel
Orville L. Pence
who are responsible

Library of Congress Catalog Card No. 67–16162
Copyright © 1967 by Scott, Foresman and Company, Glenview, Illinois 60025.
All rights reserved. Printed in the United States of America.

Regional offices of Scott, Foresman and Company are located in
Atlanta, Dallas, Glenview, Palo Alto, and Oakland, N.J.

FOREWORD

Variety is the keynote of undergraduate instruction in speech today. In some institutions of higher learning the basic speech course deals with public speaking; in others, with the fundamentals of speech; in still others, with an introduction to speech communication theory. Moreover, within these broad categories, as one moves from school to school and even from instructor to instructor within the same department, one finds that the basic speech course differs greatly in both activity and content. Subject matter that is taught in the introductory course at one institution is reserved for advanced courses at another.

One reason for this state of affairs is that the beginning undergraduate instruction in speech encompasses a wide range of subject matter—far more than can be offered in a single course. From this wealth of topics, instructors and course committees must select material that can be organized into a meaningful pattern of instruction. In addition, since the needs of students in various institutions and curricula differ considerably, textbooks that try to cover an entire semester's work have proved increasingly unable to bear the whole burden of undergraduate instruction. Writing a good survey text is further hindered by the rapid advances in knowledge and research taking place in the field. It is clear that more flexible instructional material is required.

In response to that need, Scott, Foresman's College Speech Series has been designed to provide maximum adaptibility to varying instructional goals. Our objective is to make it possible for the instructor to combine just those units of content which best serve the needs of his course: particular subject matter selected for a certain population of students at a given time. The format of the series has developed from that goal. Each title focuses on a single topic, which is developed by an "expert" in much fuller detail than is possible in a survey textbook. Each is independent of the others. The titles were chosen for minimal overlap, and no book in the series requires mastery of any other as a prerequisite for understanding. Of course, where appropriate, the authors have cross-referenced one another for purposes of fuller or more specialized treatment, so that the series, being integrated, offers a common philosophy. Each book is independent yet is also part of a consistent and comprehensive whole.

But the books of this series represent something more than a new format for instructional reading. Each provides an original analysis in depth, relying on recent theoretic advances and bringing to bear the most useful information available. The series is therefore something more than a subdivision and expansion of the typical survey textbook for the first course in speech; each book presents information and theoretical insights not heretofore available to the undergraduate student.

In some cases, it may prove desirable to build a beginning speech course around several topics selected from the series. In others, a single volume may be used to fill a void or to develop a particular topic in greater depth than does the survey textbook. Different sections of the same course may use the same general textbook but study from different volumes of this series in order to emphasize topics according to special needs. For many advanced or specialized courses, a particular book of this series may be used as the principal textbook, serving as the point of departure for extensive supplementary readings and special projects. Thus, this series may be used in a variety of ways at many different instructional levels, depending on the needs of the students, the goals of instruction, and the insight and imagination of the instructor.

Theodore Clevenger, Jr.
General Editor

CONTENTS

PREFACE

My motivation for producing this work about persuasive speaking stems from the frustrations I have experienced during my twelve years of teaching, when confronted by the diffusion of the available materials on persuasive discourse. All too many textbooks present overly generalized approaches, rely upon outdated research, and stress prescriptions rather than principles for speech behavior. Other references provide a cataloging of "hard" facts — the findings of current research on particulars — but these scholarly works seldom integrate the facts in a way which allows the student to see the "forest." Still other materials present theoretical approaches to attitude organization and change but fail to relate their descriptions of "effects" with the speech behaviors that produce those effects.

In *Persuasive Speaking* I have attempted to write a different kind of book. It is a book *about* persuasion, not a manual of prescriptive suggestions for success in persuading. The bias is that of a social scientist who is neither unmindful nor unappreciative of the contributions made by Aristotle and other classical writers on rhetoric. The emphasis is upon the *process* of persuasion, viewed as an ongoing activity, and most of our attention is devoted to the psychological-epistemological bases of the phenomenon. The persuasive speaking process is divided into phases of Receiving, Focusing, Associating, and Resolving. These phases are seen to lead to the end of persuasion, which is treated as a change in an object of judgment or a change in "meaning" for a persuadee. I have attempted not only to explain the persuasive speaking process but also to present the elements for an analysis of that process.

No attempt is made to answer every question concerning persuasive speaking: not every detail is completed, nor is every connection between thoughts spelled out in full. The reader is expected to take an active part in integrating the materials presented here and in drawing implications from them. The exercises at the end of the book are deliberately designed to help him in these tasks.

I wish to express my appreciation to the editor of this series, Theodore Clevenger, Jr., for his suggestions. And I want especially to thank my colleagues, Robert Brooks and Karl Wallace, who read the entire manuscript and offered a number of helpful comments.

Finally, my apologies to Susie and Tommy. A faculty wife has made a decision in her adult years and must accept the consequences. No child, on the other hand, deserves a faculty father who chooses to write in his spare time.

Thomas M. Scheidel

I.

THE HERITAGE

OF PERSUASIVE SPEAKING

Persuasive speaking is a topic belonging to no single period or place. A chronology of works on the subject would extend unbroken for thousands of years, throughout most of our recorded history. Persuasive speaking has occupied some of the world's most influential minds: Plato, Aristotle, Cicero, Quintilian, St. Augustine, Francis Bacon, John Quincy Adams. It has also been a subject for the pens of Niccolò Machiavelli, Vilfredo Pareto, and Adolf Hitler.

Persuasive speaking has long been a subject of study and exploration in the American university community. For fifty years teachers in departments of speech have nurtured the teaching of the theory and practice of persuasive speaking, or rhetoric, its ancient name. Today academic interest in the subject is increasing markedly, and the general topic is treated in such varied disciplines as psychology, sociology, linguistics, political science, anthropology, business and commerce, and engineering.

THE NATURE OF PERSUASIVE SPEAKING

By *persuasive speaking*, I mean that activity in which speaker and listener are conjoined and in which the speaker consciously attempts to influence the behavior of the listener by transmitting audible and visible symbolic cues.

Intent. In this book, we wish to consider only conscious and deliberate attempts to influence as persuasion. There is no doubt that one person can influence another unintentionally; but we will find it advantageous here to view such influences as something apart from persuasive speaking.

Communication. We wish to stress the element of communication – that is, the transmission and reception of symbolic cues. All that any speaker can do is to send out audible sounds in combination with factors of vocal quality and inflection, reinforced by visible postures, gestures, and facial expressions. These stimuli are received and interpreted, or given meaning, by the listener, and it is through the intermediate influence of this interpretation that the persuasive message has its effect.

Moreover, our definition stipulates that speaker and listener be conjoined. The criterion here is *joint participation* – not necessarily face-to-face interaction. While face-to-face communication is our ideal case, we would not want to exclude the mass media in which, for example, a television speaker and the television viewer would be participating jointly in the communication process, conjoined, though not in direct confrontation.

Choice. We shall speak of persuasive speaking as a phenomenon which reflects choice on the part of the listener. The listener must both choose to give his attention and choose whether or not to accept or reject the message. Brainwashing and hypnotism are possible influential techniques, and so for that matter are the use of the rack, the iron maiden, and various other devices for torture. However, such means will be considered as existing outside the limits of our definition of persuasion. Even though a listener may respond to spoken instructions while under hypnosis, or as a thumbscrew is tightened, or at gun point, we shall not consider the response due to "persuasive" speaking. We want to eliminate from our consideration all physical and super-psychological coercion, whether actual or implied. Although coercive measures are certainly classes of manipulation along with persuasive speaking, they are *not* what we call persuasive measures and should not be confused with them.

Influence. Persuasive speaking, then, is a method of influence short of any physical contact or coercion. It is effective when either the listener's observable behavior or his predispositions for behavior are modified or changed. In our treatment of this aspect, we will emphasize internal attitudinal changes, even though such changes may or may not lead to changes in observable behavior.

Persuasiveness. Consider the scope and role of persuasive speaking in our society. It occurs all about us, every day, for all purposes, and it involves all ages. Think over your activities of yesterday. How much of the time were you engaged in oral communication with the intention of exerting your influence? Total the hours in which you were speaking to others with such a purpose and in which you were listening to others (via face-to-face conversation, telephone, radio or television, film) who hoped to have some influence upon your behavior. Even your reading can be considered, since writing often is a record of what would have been spoken; although only the traces of the potential oral message are on paper, there still remains a degree of influential discourse. The hours you spent on all such discourse should represent a good portion of your day. Research on this question has demonstrated that over fifty per cent of our waking day is spent in some kind of oral communication situation, and a sizeable proportion of that time is spent uttering and listening to persuasive speaking.

The ubiquity and constancy of persuasive speaking for the individual person is only one aspect of the matter. The breadth of purpose to which it can be applied is yet another. Influential discourse is employed by small schoolchildren on the playground for negotiation, and it is used similarly by diplomats on the world scene. We see persuasive speaking used constantly for negotiating and problem solving, for advising and counseling, for cajoling and deceiving. It is a vital activity in business, politics, education, jurisprudence, and homilectics. Little wonder that it is a topic which has received attention from so many.

VIEWS OF PERSUASIVE SPEAKING

To understand persuasive speaking, it is useful to learn something about the heritage of the subject. As previously indicated, this heritage springs from so many sources and so many points of view that a summary or synthesis would be difficult at best and impossible in any brief treatment. The typical consideration of the topic, even by a single writer, tends to spread and become so encompassing that it would take many pages to summarize even a single writer's contribution with any justice.

What we shall attempt here, then, is a *sampling* of the viewpoints which have appeared. Although we will be drawing from different times and places, it is not our intent to present a history or a geography of persuasion. Rather, our single aim will be to sample the variety of treatments that have been made of the persuasive-speaking process. We will concentrate on the psychological-epistemological elements in those works; that is, our special concern will be with how the writers *explain* the occurrence and influence of persuasive speaking.

Rhetoric, or the rationale of persuasive speaking, was a central concern in the early Greek society. In this early civilization, speech was a dominant force. The extent of the oral nature of the Greek civilization is described by George Kennedy:

> Both the mechanics of ancient civilization and its primary expression remained oral. The political system, for example, operated through the direct speech of the citizens among themselves and to their magistrates, and of the magistrates to their administrative assistants. Writing was used to record a vote, a law, a resolution, but rarely to achieve it in the first place. Political agitation was usually accomplished or defeated by word of mouth. The judicial system was similarly oral: verbal complaints were brought before magistrates, who held hearings; then the litigants pleaded their own cases in public before a jury of citizens. Documents were few. There were written business contracts, but they were negotiated and enforced by face-to-face argument rather than by prolonged correspondence. There were no newspapers, magazines, handbills, or circulars; information was spread orally. Entertainment was provided only to a limited extent by reading; informal conversation, the legitimate stage, or the sound of the human voice in some form constituted the commonest form of diversion. All literature was written to be heard, and even when reading to himself a Greek read aloud.[1]

In a society which devoted such emphasis to oral discourse, it is not surprising to find a substantial body of materials on oral persuasion. Regrettably, the surviving records are often incomplete and do not provide enough understanding of the principles underlying persuasive influence. A review of a few of these principles, however, will point to some concepts, some questions, and some issues on persuasion which are important still.

The Sophist-Platonist controversy

In the middle of the fifth century B.C., certain teachers, called Sophists, claimed to prepare their pupils for civil life by providing a general education. Good liberal education, then as now, included some attention to public speaking so that a literate man would not necessarily obscure his education when he opened his mouth. These ancients believed that speech practice could be improved with training. Protagoras (c.480–c.411 B.C.), who has been called the earliest of the

1. George Kennedy, *The Art of Persuasion in Greece* (Princeton, N. J.: Princeton University Press, 1963), p. 4. This book is one of the Recommended Readings at the end of this volume. You may consult the annotation there.

Sophists, invented topics on which his pupils debated the pros and cons. Gorgias (c.485–c.380 B.C.) emphasized oral style. Hippias of Elis (c. 5th century B.C.), another Sophist, provided training in improving the memory as an essential in the preparation of an orator.

At about this same time Corax (c. 470 B.C.), a Sicilian Greek, developed what is generally considered to be the first system of persuasive principles. A major tenet advanced by Corax was that a persuader should employ arguments which seem probable (plausible). If, for example, a small man is accused of attacking a larger man, he defends himself by asking, "Is it likely that I would attack that man who is so much larger than I and who could so easily counter my attack?" If, on the other hand, a larger man is accused of attacking a smaller man, his best defense is to put the question, "Is it reasonable that I would attack that man and risk a case of assault, where the presumption is so sure to be against me?" As far as recorded advice to speakers is concerned, Corax originated the idea that probabilities persuade.

Plato (c.427–347 B.C.) attacked this form of argument in his dialogue *Phaedrus*. He condemned any suggestion that "only the probabilities should be told either in accusation or defense" or that the orator "should keep probability in view, and say good-bye to the truth." Plato's general attack upon the Sophists was so vigorous and damning that the word *sophisticated* still carries, as one of its meanings, the implication of artificiality and falsity.

But Plato's attack upon the Sophists was perhaps too extreme. Some scholars have pointed to virtues which the Sophists can justifiably claim. The Sophists were largely responsible for developing the educational system of their day. They taught their students to value oratorical and literary excellence. It has been said that their one great defect was an indifference to truth. But even in this, there was some value, for the Sophists were reacting against the concept of an *absolute* truth. Protagoras held that all things are in flux and that sensation is subjective, and he advanced the view that "man is the measure of all things." In our day, too, many reject the notion of absolute truth. But more will be said about this in the next chapter.

Plato's positive contribution to the principles of rhetoric came in the closing sections of the *Phaedrus*. There he points out that a persuader should be a philosopher and discover the truth, but he should also be a psychologist and understand human nature. He must understand how to organize and adapt materials for an audience.

Until a man knows the truth of the several particulars of which he is writing or speaking, and is able to define them as they are, and having defined them again to divide them until they can be no longer divided, and until in like manner he is able to discern the nature of the soul, and discover the different modes of discourse which are adapted to different natures, and to arrange and dispose them in such a way that the simple form of speech may be addressed to the simpler nature, and the complex and composite to the more complex nature – until he had accomplished all this, he will be unable to handle arguments according to rules or art, as far as their nature allows them to be subjected to art, either for the purpose of teaching or persuading.[2]

Desirable as such goals undeniably are, their attainment is rarely discernible. It is the evaluation of Everett Hunt that "the ideal rhetoric sketched in the *Phaedrus* is as far from the possibilities of mankind as his Republic was from Athens."[3]

The conflict between the Sophists and Plato does not help us greatly in understanding modern principles of persuasion, but it does dramatize the effect of differing assumptions about human nature and society upon one's theory of persuasion. Many of the Sophists were epistemological skeptics; they did not believe that absolute truth existed or that man could know it even if it did. Perhaps because of this view, man became the "measure of all things," and the *effectiveness* of a persuasive speech was its only standard. These assumptions led to training of a highly prescriptive nature calculated only to achieve success. Plato, on the other hand, believed in absolute truth and the possibility of obtaining it. Interestingly, his assumptions also led to specific prescriptions, but only to those in which truth is more important than success.

Evidence of Sophistic and Platonic views of persuasion is still with us. Almost every magazine one picks up in a barbershop contains advertisements offering to make you "A DYNAMIC, FORCEFUL SPEAKER WHO CAN SELL YOURSELF AND YOUR IDEAS." We are led to imagine that we will soon have more friends and admirers than we can handle and money by the bushel. These advertised courses typically provide sets of simple, straightforward directions: "Call a person by his name," "Ask about his family," and so on. The principles behind these bits of advice are not discussed; only directives are given. While in some ways it is unfair to identify these crass modern enterprisers with the Sophists, they do reflect some of the tendencies of those ancient teachers.

2. Plato, *Phaedrus*, in *The Dialogues of Plato*, trans. B. Jowett (New York: Random House, Inc., 1937), I, p. 280. Originally published by the Clarendon Press, Oxford. Interested students may wish also to read Plato's dialogue *Gorgias*.
3. Everett Lee Hunt, "Plato and Aristotle on Rhetoric and Rhetoricians," in *Historical Studies of Rhetoric and Rhetoricians*, ed. Raymond J. Howes (Ithaca: Cornell University Press, 1961), p. 54. This essay is recommended for collateral reading.

The same is true of Machiavelli (1469–1527), the Italian statesman who was noted for his philosophy of expediency. Machiavelli wrote about the methods of an absolutist leader and recommended behavior calculated to keep such a ruler in control. Another exemplar of this Sophistic tendency was Vilfredo Pareto (1848–1923), a sociologist and economist who produced *Trattato di Sociologia Generale*. This university professor, who could claim Mussolini as a pupil, contributed to the development of the Fascist viewpoint. In his work he maintained that "sentiments" (desires, interests) dominate society. Man feels called upon to explain his actions and argues himself into believing that his behavior is logical and hence justifiable. He persuades himself by means of "derivations": (1) assertions and dogmatic statements, (2) use of authority, (3) appeals to sentiments, and (4) verbal proofs.

When we speak of man as the "measure of all things," we must not neglect to mention Adolf Hitler (1889–1945). Hitler believed that all great, world-shaking events had been brought about by the spoken rather than the written word, and he made specific suggestions about speaking. Hitler commented, as did Plato, on the great advantage speaking has over writing: the speaker sees his specific and immediate audience and is able to change his approach during the course of his speech and thus adapt to the feedback he receives from his audience.

> . . . he will, if he is a brilliant popular orator, not be likely to repeat the same reproach and the same substance twice in the same form. He will always let himself be borne by the great masses in such a way that instinctively the very words come to his lips that he needs to speak to the hearts of his audience. And if he errs, even in the slightest, he has the living correction before him. As I have said, he can read from the facial expression of his audience whether, firstly, they *understand* what he is saying, whether, secondly, they can *follow the speech as a whole,* and to what extent; thirdly, he has *convinced* them of the *soundness* of what he has said.[4]

In *Mein Kampf* Hitler speaks of the effect of the atmosphere of the meeting hall and of the effect of the crowd upon the individual; he recommends night meetings because at night an audience will "succumb more easily to the dominating force of a stronger will." Hitler's standard for speech effectiveness has a decidedly sophistic ring:

4. Adolf Hitler, *Mein Kampf,* trans. Ralph Manheim, Sentry edition (Boston: Houghton Mifflin Company, 1943), pp. 470–471.

For I must not measure the speech of a statesman to his people by the impression which it leaves in a university professor, but by the effect it exerts on the people. And this alone gives the standard for the speaker's genius.[5]

While it would be somewhat misleading to call them Platonists, we do find those today who espouse the opposite extreme. These modern "Platonists" deplore the use of "psychological" appeals and insist on the complete truth. They advocate what they term "logical" appeals. For example:

It is the thesis of this entire criticism that argumentation must be taught as a process of discovering and communicating whatever truth may be discoverable in a given social controversy; and that belief and conduct, if not influenced by a presentation of *all* the facts in a given controversy, had better not be influenced at all.[6]

Can you imagine a speech or even a series of speeches that presents *all* the facts in any given social controversy? The time factor alone makes it impossible. Such intentions still are as far from being possible as is the society of Plato's *Republic*.

Aristotle

Plato's most famous pupil, Aristotle (384–322 B.C.), developed perhaps the single most influential account of rhetorical theory in the *Rhetoric*. Aristotle's influence on thought and writing about persuasion has continued for over two thousand years and still is apparent in contemporary public speaking textbooks and other writings about persuasion. His *Rhetoric* is the classic work on persuasive speaking, and anyone interested in the subject must know something of this great philosopher in order to understand the significance of the heritage he has left us.

Aristotle defined rhetoric as "the faculty of observing in any given case the available means of persuasion." He considered rhetoric to deal with the probable and the contingent, for no one deliberates about certainties. This is surely an acceptable view today, for most public issues of controversy are such that intelligent men may hold conflicting views. Such topics are judged by relative standards and not by absolutes.

---

5. Ibid., p. 477.
6. Angelo M. Pellegrini, "Argumentation and Personal Success," *Quarterly Journal of Speech*, XXIX (February 1943), 30.

Aristotle distinguished between different materials of persuasion. On the one hand, he considered the use of witnesses, written documents, and similar materials of fact and evidence. On the other hand, he considered the manner in which the speaker employs his own inventiveness.

According to Aristotle, rhetoric has four main uses. First, it is a *means for assuring the predominance of truth.* Aristotle believed that truth and justice are, by their nature, easier to accept than are untruths and injustice. Therefore, if truth is presented as skillfully as any falsehood is presented, truth will win out. Second, rhetoric provides a *means for adapting a topic* for the general audience. Third, it allows us a *means of seeing both sides of a controversial question* so that we may better understand it. Finally, it provides us with a *means of self-defense,* and Aristotle asserted that it is a more human characteristic to be able to defend oneself with speech and reason than by means of physical force.

To understand Aristotle's explanations of persuasion, we must look at the "modes of persuasion" as he outlined them:

Of the modes of persuasion furnished by the spoken word there are three kinds. The first kind depends on the personal character of the speaker; the second on putting the audience into a certain frame of mind; the third on the proof, or apparent proof, provided by the words of the speech itself. Persuasion is achieved by the speaker's personal character when the speech is so spoken as to make us think him credible. We believe good men more fully and more readily than others: this is true generally whatever the question is, and absolutely true where exact certainty is impossible and opinions are divided. This kind of persuasion, like the others, should be achieved by what the speaker says, not by what people think of his character before he begins to speak. It is not true, as some writers assume in their treatises on rhetoric, that the personal goodness revealed by the speaker contributes nothing to his power of persuasion; on the contrary, his character may almost be called the most effective means of persuasion he possesses. Secondly, persuasion may come through the hearers, when the speech stirs their emotions. Our judgements when we are pleased and friendly are not the same as when we are pained and hostile. It is towards producing these effects, as we maintain, that present-day writers on rhetoric direct the whole of their efforts. This subject shall be treated in detail when we come to speak of the emotions. Thirdly, persuasion is effected through the speech itself when we have proved a truth or an apparent truth by means of the persuasive arguments suitable to the case in question.[7]

According to Aristotle, then, there are three modes of persuasive appeal: ethos, or source credibility; emotional appeal; and logical proof.

Ethos. The first means of persuasion discussed by Aristotle is *ethos,* or the "character" of the speaker. Behavior exhibited by a speaker which is interpreted by the listener as revealing a person of high character, intelligence, and good will creates persuasive influence. Contemporary studies of *ethos* have settled upon the following elements in defining this concept operationally: (1) expertness, (2) trustworthiness, and (3) personal dynamism. Many contemporary studies have demonstrated the persuasive influence of credibility, but in most of them credibility was studied as it existed *prior* to the speech occasion rather than as it developed *during* the speech event. In such a study a tape-recorded speech is presented to two groups. One group is told that the speech was delivered by a college professor; the other group is told it was given by a college sophomore. The same speech is found to have more persuasive influence when attributed to the college professor. On the evidence of a number of such experiments, there seems to be a solid basis for believing in the effectiveness of *ethos* in persuasive speaking.

Emotional appeal. The second mode of persuasion might be labeled *emotional appeal.* As a speaker touches upon those elements which motivate behavior, the listener will respond. Therefore, the speaker must understand the psychology of his listener and adapt his case to it. Aristotle analyzed a number of emotions he considered appropriate to the audience of that day, such as anger, love, fear, pity, and envy, and then described in each case (1) how the emotion might be described, (2) the persons toward whom the emotion is typically felt, and (3) the factors which will generally create that particular emotional state. Contemporary studies by social scientists have demonstrated the persuasive effectiveness of emotional appeals, with considerable emphasis given to the role of fear appeals. A number of experimental studies have shown, for example, that a moderate fear appeal will result in changes in audience attitude.

7. Aristotle, *Rhetorica,* trans. W. Rhys Roberts, in *The Basic Works of Aristotle,* ed. Richard McKeon (New York: Random House, Inc., 1941), pp. 1329–1330. This edition contains an essay introduction to Aristotle, as well as some of Aristotle's treatises on logic, the soul, ethics, and poetics which deserve some attention by the interested reader.

The important point to note here is Aristotle's emphasis upon the activity of the *listener* in the persuasive setting: the emotional state of a listener, when stimulated, will contribute to his own persuasion. We see here an ancient root of the idea that persuasive speaking is not a one-way process in which a speaker contributes everything to the situation. Rather, persuasive speaking is an activity in which speaker and listener interact and in which both contribute to any ultimate effect. The speaker must adjust the message to the listener and the listener must participate actively in interpreting the message.

Logical appeal. Finally, in the *Rhetoric* and in other works, Aristotle discussed the proof or apparent proof inherent in the speech itself. Some persons have labeled this mode of persuasion *logical appeal.* Aristotle discussed the use of inductive and deductive reasoning in detail, but we shall merely touch upon the main features of his treatment here.

Aristotle presented the "example" as the rhetorical use of *induction;* it is the means whereby a general law is derived from a number of similar instances. In a speech a number of instances or examples are given which lead to a general statement. In a 1948 debate with Thomas E. Dewey, when both were contending for the Republican presidential nomination, Harold E. Stassen argued:

> When this present Communist party did come into power in Russia, they promptly wiped out all other political parties and took the whole peoples under a firm and dictatorial grip. In each of the other countries—Poland, Hungary, Yugoslavia, Romania, Bulgaria, Albania, and finally Czechoslovakia—the Communists used the blessing of legality as an aid to organizing an underground movement, and finally betrayed the liberties of the people and brought them under the domination of the Kremlin in Moscow.[8]

Stassen thus argued *inductively* from a number of examples to the conclusion that unless the Communist party is outlawed, it can work overground and underground to overthrow a nation and bring it under the domination of communism.

Aristotle named the "enthymeme" as the rhetorical syllogism —that is, as the principle instrument of *deduction* in persuasive discourse. We are probably all familiar with deduction, the logical form for inferring from a general premise to a specific conclusion. The most frequently cited categorical syllogism is:

8. From a tape recording of the debate broadcast by radio from Portland, Oregon.

All men are mortal.	(major premise)
Socrates is a man.	(minor premise)
Therefore, Socrates is mortal.	(conclusion)

Aristotle described the enthymeme as this syllogistic or deductive proof as it appears in persuasive speaking, where one of the premises usually goes unexpressed. It is rare, if ever, that we hear an argument stated in the complete form just given. In a speech the deductive form more likely would be:

Socrates is a man and therefore mortal.
Or:
Socrates is mortal because he is a man.

The enthymeme deals with probabilities, can be an abbreviated form of the syllogism, and may draw premises from the listeners. That is, in the interaction between persuader and persuadee, both participants may contribute premises which, taken together, lead to the inference at which the persuader is driving. In the two examples immediately above, the speaker assumes and the listener must supply for himself the omitted premise.

While Aristotle does not provide all the answers appropriate for our day, he does consider nearly all the questions: what is the influence of the speaker's character, how do speaker and listener interact in the persuasive setting, and with what concepts should we view speaker, message, and audience? Unfortunately, the great lack in Aristotle, for one searching for a more scientific theory of persuasive speaking, is the absence of explanation. He *labeled* the elements and activities but did not explain, in terms which are helpful today, how these factors lead to influence. For the contemporary theorist, Aristotle's great utility comes from the breadth of his treatment and the concepts he developed. One could hardly be considered literate on the topic of persuasive speaking without an acquaintance with the man and his ideas.

Classical rhetorical canons

The concern with persuasive speaking shown by the Sophists, Plato, and Aristotle extended well beyond these Greek originators. In Rome, Cicero (106–43 B.C.) wrote a number of related works, including *De Inventione, De Oratore, Orator, Brutus,* and *De Partitione Oratoria.* Cicero is also credited by some as being the author of the influential *Rhetorica ad Herennium,* a technical treatise on public speaking, which appeared about 82 B.C. Quintilian (35–95 A.D.) developed a system for the total education of a speaker in the *Institutio Oratoria.* Out of all the classical tradition of rhetoric came five principal divisions of the topic, or canons of rhetoric. This analysis of the general topic endured for two thousand years and still provides a tolerably accurate outline of the speaker's task. The canons were labeled *invention, disposition, elocution* or *style, delivery,* and *memory.* Let us consider each canon briefly.

Invention. The first and most important canon is *invention.* This canon covers the analysis of the proposition, the gathering and selecting of materials, and the formulation of approaches to be used. The speaker must first marshal all the facts of his case: he must gather the evidence. Then he must study the issues involved—those main and essential points upon which the opponents in an argument on the topic would clash. He must determine what these issues are and which ones he should emphasize in making his case. On some propositions, the speaker's greatest task is to convince his audience that a problem does exist. On other topics, a problem's existence may be generally accepted, and the speaker's task then is to give strong support to the specific solution he advocates.

Subordinate to invention is the rhetorical concept of "status," which has to do with a speaker's awareness of audience needs and expectations on the proposition. On what does the matter hinge? Which point demands the greatest consideration? Finally, the speaker must survey all the possible approaches and settle upon the best available means of persuasion.

Another major concept subordinate to invention is that of the "topics," or the places of arguments. Some topics are general and can serve as potential considerations for any proposition. One such topic is "cause and effect." On almost any question for discussion, one might ask, "What was the cause of this problem?" or, "What effects can we expect if this problem is not solved?" Other topics are more specific, suited to particular cases and situations. One topic for the law courts is "justice and injustice." The topics, then, are lists of possible lines of argument. They aid the speaker in the invention process. By taking up the topics in turn and by thinking about what bearing each point might have on his case, the speaker gains two advantages: (1) he is able to choose the most effective possible arguments and materials, and (2) he is prevented to a large degree from overlooking potential arguments.

Thus we see that rhetorical inventiveness consists in knowing the correct questions to ask. Some are questions about the status of the proposition; others consider the appropriateness of various topics. These questions assist the speaker in viewing his subject from a number of different reference points and guide him in selecting possible means of persuasion. We will want to say more about status and the topics later.

Disposition. The second rhetorical canon is *disposition*. Essentially, disposition concerns the order and arrangement of the speech materials. Some classical rhetorical works were quite detailed in labeling the parts of a speech. In the *Rhetorica ad Herennium*, for example, six divisions of a judicial speech are listed. Plato's account was simpler and perhaps adequate. He described speech order in the following terms: "there should be a middle, beginning, and end, adapted to one another and to the whole."

The ancients offered some general advice on where to position the strongest arguments in a forensic speech or legalistic argument. They also advised on matters such as moving from general to specific arguments. The overall view, however, seems to have been that arrangement must be governed by the specific purpose of the speech. Classical writers further admonished a speaker to adapt to his audience by making any changes dictated by its mood or disposition.

Modern investigators, too, have given attention to disposition. Researchers in speech and in psychology have studied order-and-arrangement effects. To the extent that this research has been intended as a check on theory, it is desirable. But many of the studies have been described as if their purpose was to produce a single finding applicable to all speeches. Such an intention seems futile, and, from that point of view, the results have been unproductive. There is no absolute governing whether the strongest argument should be placed first or last in a speech. We would do better to look for broad principles than to seek specific prescriptions for speaking behavior which apply in all cases. This was a point which classical rhetoricians understood.

Elocution. The third canon of classical rhetoric is *elocution*, or style. All matters of language were considered under elocution: the choice of words and the arrangement of words into larger units. As a canon, elocution has played a major role in the history of rhetoric.

Most rhetoricians have given some attention to style, and a few have devoted themselves entirely to the subject. A number of works have been produced with the sole task of cataloging the multitude of possible stylistic devices, "figures" and "tropes." Thomas Gibbons, for example, described in detail the tropes identified as "metaphor" and "allegory," as "metonymy" and "synecdoche," as "hyperbole" and "catachresis," et cetera, et cetera, et cetera.[9]

But the classical rhetoricians and their followers did not limit themselves to cataloging stylistic devices; they also tried to develop principles for evaluating stylistic excellence. Traditionally, four virtues of style were discussed: (1) Is the language correct—does it fit the accepted patterns of the educated? (2) Is the style clear, direct, and unambiguous? (3) Is the language embellished, polished, noble, moving? (4) Is the language appropriate—suited to the subject matter, audience, and speaker? The ancients further described and exemplified three levels of style: the grand (magnificent, elevated, lofty language), the middle, and the plain (simple, unadorned language).

Although we have said earlier that invention is the most important canon, its preëminence has been challenged occasionally by style. Donald Clark tells us that by the late Middle Ages, *rhetoric* had come to mean style alone.[10] To be sure, we would not want to leave the impression that invention and style are opposing canons, so that embracing one necessarily implies rejecting the other. It is true, however, that at times interest in one has prevailed at the expense of the other. But when a full and balanced account of rhetoric is attempted, invention and style are both present and wedded in the final product.

Delivery. The fourth canon was *delivery.* According to Cicero, "Delivery is the one dominant power in oratory." Cicero's assertion is extreme but not without support. The ancients' theory of delivery covered all aspects of voice and the physical elements of speaking, gesture, posture, and movement; for speakers, then as now, were aware of the importance of these matters. We are told, for instance, that Demosthenes improved his articulation by practicing speeches with pebbles in his mouth. He is also reported to have broken the habit of shrugging his shoulders by practicing his speech with a spear directly over his shoulder. (To our knowledge, neither of these practices is widely recommended today.) Speakers were advised to give attention to voice and articulation, to avoid monotony and a rate of delivery either too fast or too slow. They were advised to use gestures, but not excessively, to maintain good posture, and to refrain from random movement.

9. Thomas Gibbons, *Rhetoric,* in *Selected Readings in Rhetoric and Public Speaking,* ed. Lester Thonssen (New York: The H. W. Wilson Company, 1942), pp. 219–230. This book contains selections from many older rhetorical works not readily available to the reader.

10. Donald L. Clark, *Rhetoric in Greco-Roman Education* (New York: Columbia University Press, 1957), p. 83. This work is highly recommended. See Recommended Readings for comment.

A few writers seem to have made too much of delivery. Whole works have been produced on the "art of the gesture." One account by Gilbert Austin presents a catalog of gestures and postures.[11] We are told that the palm of the hand may be positioned in one of the following manners: prone, supine, inwards, outwards, forwards, backwards, vertical. The eyes may be: directed forward, averted, looking upwards, round, vacant. John Bulwer, in his *Chirologia*, informs the reader:

> *The Fore-Finger Put Forth, The Rest Contracted To A Fist*, is an expresse of *command* and *direction;* a gesture of the *Hand* most *demonstrative.*
>
> *To Bend The Middle-Finger While It Stifly Resteth Upon The Thumb, And So In Restingwise To Let It Off*, a triviall expression whereby we with a *Fillip inflict a trifling punishment*, or *a scoffe.*[12]

Many of these prescriptions bring smiles today. Yet the fact remains that by and large the bulk of the general suggestions on delivery in most rhetorical sources has some basis in the accepted standards of the culture in which and for which each was produced.

Memory. The final canon is that of *memory.* The speaker in ancient times was given instruction for developing his memory. Often this was done by a mnemonic device based on visual association; that is, the speaker was to associate the sequence of his arguments with physical and visual objects known to him in some well-established order. These associations then would prompt his recall of the points in proper sequence. Memory is the only canon which has been dropped from most modern speech textbooks. Although the vocabulary and examples have changed, traces of the other canons are to be found in almost any current work on persuasive speaking.

The remark made earlier about Aristotle's contribution will fit the classical rhetorical canons as well. He and other classical writers introduced proper concepts and raised important first questions. Their prescriptions, although often too specific, generally are sound and well advised. But their weaknesses lie in the absence of explanation. Why is it that the suggestions *are* sound? Why is it that they *do* work? We are not told how the prescriptions for the speaker's behavior lead to persuasive influence in the audience. And the principles of influence are what we must have if we are to understand the persuasive-speaking process fully.

11. Gilbert Austin, *Chironomia*, in *Selected Readings*, pp. 263–279.
12. John Bulwer, *Chirologia*, in *Selected Readings*, pp. 197–198.

One could review the works by rhetoricians from classical times to the present without adding significantly to what has already been outlined. Although in 1828 Richard Whately, Archbishop of Dublin, may have considered himself exempt from his own criticism, even today we might accept his statement that rhetoric

> is not one of those branches of study in which we can trace with interest a progressive improvement from age to age. It is one, on the contrary, to which more attention appears to have been paid, and in which greater proficiency is supposed to have been made, in the earliest days of science and literature, than at any subsequent period. Among the ancients, Aristotle, the earliest whose works are extant, may safely be pronounced to be also the best of the systematic writers on Rhetoric.[13]

Modern approaches to persuasion

The knowledge explosion touched off by the Renaissance had by the opening of the twentieth century made it practically impossible for any one individual to assimilate more than a fragment of the available information about mankind, the arts, and the sciences. Consequently, learning became more specialized under such new headings as "physics," "psychology," "political science," and the like. "Rhetoric" retained a measure of its identity through its continuing contact with the classical writers, but many of its traditional concerns were taken over by the newly emerging specialties, especially by psychology. Accordingly, two distinct threads are present in the fabric of modern persuasion theory: (1) the rhetorical, promulgated in modern departments of speech, and (2) the psychological, promulgated in modern departments of psychology. These two threads are so closely intertwined that it is sometimes impossible to untangle them, and each has contributed much to the other; but they do represent approaches which are sufficiently distinct to warrant discussing them separately. We shall consider the modern speech approaches first, then take up modern psychological approaches to persuasion.

Modern rhetorical approaches. The treatment of persuasion by teachers of speech since 1900, revealed primarily in textbooks for college and university courses, has tended to follow the classical canons, at least in broad outline. Aside from suggestions for rehearsal, the canon of memory is generally not treated, and there is

13. Richard Whately, *Elements of Rhetoric* (Nashville, Tenn.: Southern Methodist Publishing House, 1861), p. 20.

perhaps too little emphasis on the element of choice in invention. Perhaps we can clarify this latter comment. Most textbook treatments are adequate on the matter of gathering materials, and the admonishment and advice they give to that end are helpful. But the concept of status often goes unmentioned, and suggestions concerning audience analysis and adaptation usually tend to be so general as to be of little help. More good work is needed to provide speakers with a modern system of *topoi* (the previously mentioned "topics" or lists of possible lines of arguments) to assist them in making choices during the invention process. Which of the available materials should be used for a given audience at a given moment? Which issue is now pressing for this audience? Apart from these mentioned deviations, however, the texts follow the classical pattern and are usually strongest in their treatment of the canons of organization, style, and delivery.

Throughout the last forty years research scholars in speech have conducted descriptive and experimental studies of persuasion, many of which are recorded in the *Quarterly Journal of Speech* and in *Speech Monographs*. This research has emphasized the topics of stage fright or speech fear, the effects of using evidence and other speech materials, language, the *ethos* of a speaker, speech organization, and the process of persuasion generally. The findings of these studies have been slow in making their way into the persuasion textbooks. In this field, as in others, the textbook writer frequently has failed to draw upon the most recently available research findings. Even greater than this weakness is the repeated failure to incorporate the available theory or explanation of the phenomenon into the work. One often hears the complaint that too many speech texts are manuals of prescriptive directives telling the reader "how to do," rather than an exposition of principles "about" the phenomenon.

However, some of the better works have attempted the type of explanation needed. James A. Winans, Professor of Public Speaking at Cornell University, produced his influential *Public Speaking* in 1915. Winans followed the classical canons, except for memory, and borrowed from his contemporaries in psychology, Cornell's E. B. Tichener and Harvard's William James. Winans based his explanation of influential discourse on the concept of *attention*, beginning with James' assertion, "What holds attention determines action." He discussed the manner in which motives and knowledge relate to attention. At the same time, he considered the ways in which the *novel*, the *familiar*, the *concrete*, and the *specific* contribute to attention and explored the manner of advantageously associating a speech topic with other areas of listener interest. He advanced some original thoughts on ways by which a speaker attends to his own topic. His general explanation of persuasion is summarized thus:

> To persuade a man, there seems to be nothing more or less than to win his undivided attention to the desired conduct, to make him think of that and stop thinking of other courses, or of any inhibiting ideas. . . . Persuasion is the process of inducing others to give fair, favorable, or undivided attention to propositions.[14]

William Norwood Brigance presented an explanation which he termed a *genetic* approach to persuasion. He advanced the view that "The tools of persuasion are best understood and most effectively used if we view them in the order of their origin and development in the race." We might best use Brigance's own summary of his explanation of rhetorical influence:

> The acceptance of ideas borrowed and ready-made, which we call Authority, is the oldest mode of persuasion in the human race. It is still the most potent with primitive man; still highly potent with the masses; and becomes less effective as we go up the educational and intellectual scale. *To use persuasion at this level, the speaker seeks to establish a Personal Prestige; or if this be inadequate, to identify himself with some institution, or organization (political, religious, etc.) of recognized Authority. Thus fortified, he may rely upon Assertion and Suggestion — he may indeed speak with the Voice of a Prophet.*
> The second mode of persuasion acquired in the human race was the acceptance of ideas that fit into organized and ordered Experience. It is potent at all levels of society. *To use persuasion at this level, the speaker assembles his picture with materials familiar to the hearer — by colorful words and effective phrases, by figures of speech and interrogation, by illustration and comparison. While the picture is builded, he cements attention by the devices of activity and suspense.*
> The most recently acquired mode of persuasion in the race is Reason. It is the newest, therefore the weakest. It is ineffective among primitive peoples; almost equally ineffective among the lowest stratum of civilized peoples. It is safe for the common man only upon familiar ground. *To use persuasion at this level, the speaker will judiciously mix it with Authority and Experi-*

14. James A. Winans, *Public Speaking* (New York: The Century Company, 1921), p. 194.

ence, except in addressing persons of the highest intellectual level.[15]

Although Brigance's genetic theory of persuasion is interesting, the findings of more current research would argue against it. However, it is noteworthy from an historical point of view because it represents an effort to *explain* persuasive effects by means of a general theory.

Yet another explanation of persuasion is presented by Winston Brembeck and William Howell in their *Persuasion: A Means of Social Control.*[16] They defined persuasion as "the conscious attempt to modify thought and action by manipulating the motives of men toward predetermined ends." Their treatment was largely eclectic in that it drew together numerous theoretical approaches and empirical findings from various fields of knowledge. They did provide a measure of unity to their approach by focusing upon *motivation* and the process of *association* implicit in their definition. In essence, they treated persuasive influence as the process of associating the desired proposition with currently salient motives of the audience.

In even more modern treatments of speech, we see attempts to add to our understanding of persuasive speaking. The major classical canons still tend to be central, although the concepts are refined and details added. Research findings are slowly but steadily making an impression upon our texts. The current research work, as a body, is probably making its best contribution by refining concepts and by describing the persuasive process with increasing and narrowing precision.

Modern psychological approaches. Much of the current contribution to our knowledge of persuasion is made by psychologists interested in the persuasive process. Some of this research is less valuable than it might be, due to a general reluctance of each generation to look back to the work of its predecessors. Consequently, research questions are sometimes ill-formulated, research is done on relatively obsolete questions, and "new" explanatory principles turn out to be old explanations merely cast in new and often less satisfactory language. In a few instances, contributors from this area seem strangely unaware of any writing on persuasion done prior to 1900 or occasionally even prior to 1940. Nevertheless, the burgeoning of modern psychology has given rise to many valuable insights into the process of persuasion.

15. William Norwood Brigance, "A Genetic Approach to Persuasion," *Quarterly Journal of Speech*, XVII (June 1931), 329–339. Reprinted by permission of Speech Association of America.
16. This work is included in the Recommended Readings.

One well-organized psychological assault on the complexities of persuasive influence was directed by the late Carl Hovland at Yale University. Hovland's group has produced a series of books and dozens of research articles related to persuasion. The earliest research by this group is summarized in the volume *Communication and Persuasion* by Hovland, Janis, and Kelley. The work has a solid theoretical base which relies on a stimulus-response learning theory and psychoanalytic motivational theory. Persuasion is understood to be divisible into three "internal mediating subprocesses": *attention, comprehension,* and *acceptance.* The major contribution of *Communication and Persuasion,* however, is probably not so much its theoretical development as it is the results of the studies done, the specific findings. Some of the lines of inquiry opened up by this research have been most productive.

One finding of great interest to students of persuasion is the "sleeper effect." It had been found, as we have long known, that a speaker's prestige or lack of it would add to or diminish his persuasive influence. A high-prestige source will be more influential than a low-prestige source even if they present identical messages. But examining the long-term effects of persuasive messages led to some surprises. The sleeper effect names the phenomenon whereby a source and a message become disassociated as time passes and the influence of the source is separated from the influence of the message. In some cases, when a low-prestige persuader presented a message, the persuasive effect (change in attitude) immediately following the speech was *less* than the persuasive effect when measured several weeks after the speech presentation. The explanation was that the negative effect of the low-prestige speaker was lost as time passed and the audience no longer associated that speaker so strongly with that point of view.

Another provocative aspect of the Yale program had to do with the effects of "active participation" in persuasion. It was found that a speaker is influenced by his own speech; that is, as a person frames the wording and expresses an idea, *even in cases when he may not agree with the thought,* he nonetheless tends to be influenced by it. This effect reportedly occurs in "brainwashing" when the subject is rewarded for giving speeches expressing ideas contrary to his own viewpoint. He does so, thinking that no one will take him seriously and there will be no harm. But an internalizing effect may occur, and the act of participation may in itself influence the speaker without his being aware of it. Thus, one of the explanations for the observed greater influence of taking part in a small-group discussion over listening to a lecture is the overt and active participation by all participants in the former.

These findings, along with the results of intensive investigation of the effects of fear appeals on persuasive influence and on personality characteristics related to susceptibility to persuasive influence, are some of the more interesting contributions of the Yale studies. However, as stated in one of the earlier Yale volumes:

> The research findings available so far have not led to any great sharpening of theoretical constructs, and they frequently lend themselves to alternative interpretations. In other words, research in this field has not yet reached the stage where precise theoretical questions can be put to the data; thus none of the existing studies can be regarded as *crucial* research with respect to testing rival theories.[17]

Other psychologists have been moved more to attempt theory-building or explanation concerning persuasive influence. The consistency theories based on some type of cognitive model certainly represent one current vogue,[18] and a number of such explanations have been proposed. The general view of these theories is that we are all motivated to achieve a balance or harmony among our "cognitions." Cognition is taken here to cover all our knowledge, beliefs, and judgments about ourselves or our environment. If anything should create an imbalance or state of dissonance, then we are motivated to adjust our cognitions to achieve a *new* balance. Since this viewpoint has been employed to explain changes in attitude resulting from persuasive appeals, it will prove worthwhile to examine briefly one of the consistency theories.

We will consider here the "congruity" approach of Osgood and Tannenbaum. The formal statement of the congruity principle is:

> *Whenever two signs are related by an assertion, the mediating reaction characteristic of each shifts toward congruence with that characteristic of the other, the magnitude of the shift being inversely proportional to intensities of the interacting reactions.*[19]

A specific example no doubt will help clarify this formal statement. To test the principle, sources (speakers, writers) who were judged by

17. *Personality and Persuasibility*, ed. Irving L. Janis and Carl I. Hovland (New Haven: Yale University Press, 1959), pp. 25–26.
18. A good review of "balance" models is available as Chapter 11, "The Principle of Consistency in Attitude Change," in Roger Brown, *Social Psychology* (New York: The Free Press of Glencoe, Inc., 1965).
19. Charles E. Osgood, George J. Suci, and Percy H. Tannenbaum, *The Measurement of Meaning* (Urbana: University of Illinois Press, 1957), pp. 200–201.

a group of subjects as varying along a scale from positive to negative were positively and negatively associated with concepts which also varied from positive to negative. For example, one could produce an experimental message in which former President Eisenhower (positive source here) supposedly speaks against (negative association) a proposal to improve higher education (positive concept). In such a case, if a speaker we respect (+) speaks against (−) a proposal we favor (+), our cognitive balance should be upset, and we should be motivated to adjust our evaluations of source and concept in order to strike a new balance. We might see Eisenhower as somewhat less favorable but also see the proposal for higher education as somewhat less favorable. If Eisenhower were to speak against communism, our cognitive balance would *not* be upset. If he (+) spoke in favor of (+) a policy we oppose (−), then the balance again *would* be upset, and attitude change might occur. We would likely respect Eisenhower a little less and favor the proposal somewhat more.

Actually, the findings on consistency theory create some imbalance in their own right. In some cases, the data seem to fit the theory remarkably well; in others, they fail to support it. Most scholars in persuasion are uncertain yet just how to balance this matter in their own thinking.

Let us consider another contribution of modern psychology to persuasion theory. In his "summative" theory of attitude change,[20] Martin Fishbein suggests that an individual holds many *beliefs* (probabilistic aspects) toward any given psychological object. An individual believes, at some level of probability, in the existence of an object; and he believes, also at varying levels of probability, that certain elements are associated with that object. Apart from the belief structure, an individual has *affects* (evaluative aspects) toward those associated elements. The sum of all the belief elements multiplied with their associated affective quantities makes up the individual's total attitude toward the object under consideration. According to this theory, persuasion can be accomplished either by changing the belief structure of the individual or by modifying his affects concerning the object of persuasion.

Consider the total attitude of one individual toward Negroes. According to Fishbein, this person would hold a number of beliefs:

Negroes have dark skin. (belief level = .95)
Negroes are lazy. (belief level = .50)
Negroes are intellectually inferior. (belief level = .00)
And so on.

20. See Fishbein's paper, "A Consideration of Beliefs, Attitudes, and Their Relationship," in *Current Studies in Social Psychology*, ed. Ivan D. Steiner and Martin Fishbein (New York: Holt, Rinehart & Winston, Inc., 1965), pp. 107–120.

Each of the associated terms has an affective value for the individual:

Dark skin. (affective level = .40)
Laziness. (affective level = .05)
Intellectually inferior. (affective level = .00)
And so on.

The total attitude of the individual toward Negroes, then, is the sum of the belief-affect products for all beliefs-affects held:

BELIEF-AFFECT TERM	BELIEF LEVEL		AFFECT LEVEL		PRODUCT
Dark Skin	.95	×	.40	=	.380
Lazy	.50	×	.05	=	.025
Intellectually Inferior	.00	×	.00	=	.000
And so on	. . .		. . .		. . .

Total Attitude = .380 + .025 + .000 + . . . (all other products)

Although this conceptual system has been presented before, Fishbein's own measurement procedure is new, and tests thus far give this summative hypothesis some support.

Muzafer Sherif has proposed an explanation of attitude change based on ego-involvement. His view follows lengthy investigation of judgmental processes, particularly of social judgments. He has pointed out that the boundaries along the continuum from acceptance to rejection of a proposal vary for different individuals. He discusses latitudes of acceptance and rejection, asserting that "latitudes of acceptance and rejection vary with degree of familiarity, the extremity of the individual's stand, and the degree of ego-involvement with the issue." His explanation seems to fit the findings of numerous studies of persuasion fairly well. Sherif suggests that:

> With relative lack of familiarity, categories of acceptance and rejection are rather undifferentiated owing to the lack of an intensely held stand. For purposes of change through communication, the situation is favorable.[21]

If an individual is extremely and intensely favorable to a position,

> . . . the problem of changing the individual's position through communication is exceedingly difficult. Even a communication

21. Muzafer Sherif and Carl I. Hovland, *Social Judgment* (New Haven: Yale University Press, 1961), p. 193.

designed to present a moderate point of view may be regarded by the recipient with an extremely "pro" stand as being somewhat "con" in its approach. The advocated position falls squarely within his latitude of rejection and, far from convincing him, the communication is more likely to reinforce his own entrenched stand.[22]

And finally,

. . . we may say that the wider the latitude of acceptance for positions on an issue, the greater the probability of producing opinion change through communication. In addition, the greater the ego-involvement with an issue on which the individual has an established attitude, the narrower the latitude of acceptance and, consequently, the less the likelihood of opinion change through communication.[23]

In a more recent presentation of Sherif's approach, the following summary statement is made:

A change in attitude, therefore, implies a change in his [the persuadee's] categories for evaluation, which amounts to changing a part of himself; and it implies manifest change in the patterned behaviors from which they are inferred. The frame of reference for studying attitude change, therefore, includes the individual's stand and his degree of involvement in it, which affects the extent to which it is the major anchor in a communication situation. It includes the communication itself, its form, and the order of arguments. It includes the communicator and the source, both of which affect the extent to which the position presented in communication anchors the individual's subsequent appraisals of the issue. Thus, a source and speaker with high standing or prestige in the person's eyes, in effect, enhances the anchoring function of the advocated position. Similarly, any event or procedure that successfully involves the individual in a position presented to him, such as the necessity of doing a good job of presenting it or defending it himself, increases the salience of that position as an anchor when he subsequently evaluates the issue.[24]

The similarities between Sherif's views and my own approach to persuasion will be noted in later chapters. Especially relevant is the

22. Ibid., pp. 194–195.
23. Ibid., p. 196.
24. Carolyn W. Sherif, Muzafer Sherif, and Roger E. Nebergall, *Attitude and Attitude Change: The Social Judgment-Involvement Approach* (Philadelphia: W. B. Saunders Company, 1965), pp. 242–243.

opening statement in the preceding paragraph—that a change in attitude amounts, in fact, to a change in the *person* of the persuadee.

/ Daniel Katz has made an important contribution to the theory of persuasion with his presentation of a functional approach to the study of attitudes. He suggests that attitudes perform four major functions for an individual: (1) an adjustive or instrumental function, (2) an ego-defensive function, (3) a value-expressive function, and (4) a knowledge function. Katz's schematic account of the origins and the arousal and change conditions for the various functions is presented on the opposite page.[25]

From this chart, it will be apparent that Katz's approach should be helpful to one attempting an analysis of almost any persuasive message. In a trial application, look at the column listing "Arousal Conditions" and see if you can guess what types of speech appeal would lead to the arousal of the four types of attitude functions.

In summary we can see that the modern psychologist has added materially to the specifics of our understanding of the persuasive process and is beginning to make substantial theoretical contributions explaining that process.

Expanding interest. Persuasion is a phenomenon which has caught the attention of scholars in all ages and representing divergent viewpoints and approaches. We have attempted here to sketch a number of the major features of the rich heritage of persuasive discourse and to touch upon a few of the contemporary viewpoints. We recognize that the danger in such a sampling is that one might interpret it as pretending to be a summary, but we emphasize that this has not been our purpose.

We have not, for example, touched here on the work of Kenneth Burke, who makes *identification* the key term of persuasion. Burke's development of the concepts of identification and of consubstantiality, as well as his pentad of terms for analysis of human behavior (act, scene, agent, agency, purpose), are important contributions to persuasive theory; and we will draw upon some of these concepts later.[26] Neither have we space here to treat the emphasis that I. A. Richards gives to language in the process of influential discourse; but our emphasis upon language and man's categorizing process will be evident in the next chapter.

The English philosopher, logician, and author of *The Uses of Argument*, Stephen Toulmin, has made important strides in applying

25. Daniel Katz, "The Functional Approach to the Study of Attitudes," *The Public Opinion Quarterly*, XXIV (Summer 1960), 192. Reprinted by permission of the publisher.

26. Citations for Burke and the other new names presented in the next few paragraphs will be presented when the works of these scholars are taken up in more detail in later chapters.

FUNCTION	ORIGIN AND DYNAMICS	AROUSAL CONDITIONS	CHANGE CONDITIONS
Adjustment	Utility of attitudinal object in need satisfaction. Maximizing external rewards and minimizing punishments	1. Activation of needs 2. Salience of cues associated with need satisfaction	1. Need deprivation 2. Creation of new needs and new levels of aspiration 3. Shifting rewards and punishments 4. Emphasis on new and better paths for need satisfaction
Ego defense	Protecting against internal conflicts and external dangers	1. Posing of threats 2. Appeals to hatred and repressed impulses 3. Rise in frustrations 4. Use of authoritarian suggestion	1. Removal of threats 2. Catharsis 3. Development of self-insight
Value expression	Maintaining self-identity; enhancing favorable self-image; self-expression and self-determination	1. Salience of cues associated with values 2. Appeals to individual to reassert self-image 3. Ambiguities which threaten self-concept	1. Some degree of dissatisfaction with self 2. Greater appropriateness of new attitude for the self 3. Control of all environmental supports to undermine old values
Knowledge	Need for understanding, for meaningful cognitive organization, for consistency and clarity	1. Reinstatement of cues associated with old problem or of old problem itself	1. Ambiguity created by new information or change in environment 2. More meaningful information about problems

a "logical" model to the arguments of the real world. While in many respects his layout of arguments resembles the classical *epicheireme,* his reformulation is helpful. Our desire to analyze man's logical nature has always been confounded by our bias that he *must* be so. Chaïm Perelman of the University of Brussels is another philosopher who has turned his attentions to the renewed interest in rhetoric. He brings the full scope of rhetorical thought, from the *Rhetorica ad Herennium* to Solomon Asch, to bear on his analysis of the rhetorical act.

While in many ways it seems incongruous to mention the work of the Madison Avenue advertising agencies in the company of these scholars, we all know of the advertiser's pragmatic interest in persuasion. With the use of the survey, depth interview and trial-and-error attempts, these persuaders have been able in some cases to promote products which are no better than their competition. The *explanation* of persuasive influence from these sources, however, seems largely to come after the fact; and such *post hoc* explanations provide a notoriously weak basis for the development of a predictive theory. These advertisers may have found that attractive packaging helps sell products, but we can perhaps take comfort from the fact that this *post hoc* explanatory approach also produced the Edsel (if you know what an Edsel was).

In this chapter we have defined persuasive speaking as that activity in which speaker and listener are conjoined and in which the speaker consciously attempts to influence the listener by transmitting audible and visible symbolic cues. We have defined and discussed the terms of this definition in the hope of making our position clear. We have repeatedly emphasized the widespread and enduring interest in the subject of persuasion. There should be no need to labor the point further. Our hope is that the sampling of views presented thus far, ranging from the Aristotelian modes of persuasion and the classical rhetorical canons to contemporary theoretical formulations and experimental approaches, will serve to provide a better appreciation of the rhetorical heritage as well as a basis for the discussion that follows.

2.

ANTECEDENTS TO

PERSUASIVE SPEAKING

Before we can begin to understand the persuasive speaking process, we need to examine the nature of man in his environment and the way he arrives at propositions to which he will attempt to persuade others. In short, we must focus upon the antecedents to persuasive speaking. As Plato admonished in his dialogue *Phaedrus*, "Since it is in fact the function of speech to influence souls [minds], a man who is going to be a speaker must know how many types of souls there are." The following discussion of certain aspects of the nature of man will be brief and general; no effort will be made to account for every conceivable aspect of human behavior. Rather, we shall sketch out those features of human nature especially relevant to the act of persuasive speaking and the response to it.

PREDICTABILITY AND CHANGE IN THE ENVIRONMENT

How would one describe the nature of the world in which we live? There was a time not long ago when the world was viewed by some as relatively stable and static. Less than two hundred years ago, Pierre Simon de Laplace, a French scientist, held that everything that happens in the universe is the mechanically necessary result of what has gone before and necessarily determines what will come to pass in the future. Order and regularity seemed to prevail. From this view, nothing "new" was expected. The world was viewed as determined and determinable, like the freely swinging pendulum with its regular, uniform, predictable beats.

The modern view of the universe is very different. William James, famous American philosopher and Harvard professor of psychology at the turn of the century, described the baby's universe as "one big blooming, buzzing confusion." The existentialist philosopher of today might describe the universe of man similarly, and much of the modern philosophy of science would lend support to that description. The Heisenberg Principle of Indeterminacy makes it clear that man cannot even hypothetically achieve complete scientific precision; uncertainty is still a certainty for us. In this atomic age most of us know how the Geiger-Müller counter reacts to particles or rays emitted by the disintegration of radioactive atoms. Unlike the regular beats of a pendulum, the clicks heard on the Geiger counter occur at irregular, random intervals. The physical world, as detected here, no longer appears uniformly ordered and regular. Scientists such as Norbert Wiener and Nobel Prize winner Arthur Compton have told us that no kind of observation can be made which will allow an exact prediction of an atomic event.[1] We are told by scientists that our universe is constantly expanding and evolving; that entropy, or uncertainty and randomness, is steadily increasing; and that the whole process is irreversible. In these terms, the universe no longer appears ordered, regular, stable, and determinable. So, while agreeing with William James that a baby is born to confusion, we would add the view that man must live within it.

While witnessing an increase in the complexity of our physical world, we also see an increase in the complexity of our social world. Increasing population, increasing technology, increasing knowledge interact to produce, among other things, an increasingly complex social order. Social problems, about which one might speak persuasively to another, are becoming more and more complicated. Simple solutions are becoming fewer and fewer. As we add radioactive particles to our atmosphere, detergents to our water supply, and expressways and subdivisions to our land, innumerable new problems are created for which solutions must be sought. And if these problems are to be resolved, some measure of influential discourse or persuasive speaking will likely be involved.

The view of our environment advanced here is current, and yet it is not startlingly new or different. The philosopher Heraclitus, five centuries before the birth of Christ, taught that all things are in a state of flux, that existence is change. We are saying that man's universe is dynamic, evolving, constantly changing, and to a certain

1. See, for example: Arthur H. Compton, "Science and Man's Freedom," *The Atlantic Monthly* CC (October 1957), 71–74; Norbert Wiener, *Cybernetics*, 2nd ed. (New York: M.I.T. Press and John Wiley & Sons, Inc., 1961), pp. 92–94; Hans Reichenbach, *The Rise of Scientific Philosophy* (Berkeley: University of California Press, 1957).

extent unpredictable. Just as no two fingerprints are exactly alike, so it is true that no two entities or objects in the world are exactly alike. However slowly, every individual entity is changing and evolving, so that at any given moment no object is exactly as it was or exactly as it will be.

The uncertainty which is central in this viewpoint could be defeating for an individual. If so little is certain, how are we to arrive at propositions in which we can have enough confidence to dare attempt to influence others, whether by persuasion or by any other means? My answer would be, first, that the humility and self-doubt engendered by this view are altogether healthy and desirable; and, second, that the challenge of living in this existence makes being human worthwhile. For man is admirably designed to function in a changing world, and it is only when we cease to view our world as static and think of our environment as a dynamic process that we can hope to understand man's behavior. Now let us consider some of the ways in which man behaves in this existence.

MAN ADAPTS TO HIS ENVIRONMENT

Man's behavior is adaptive. This is one of the first characteristics to be noticed of human behavior. Each person adjusts himself to his world and that world to himself. Much of this adaptive behavior doubtless is necessary for survival of self and species. The human being is driven by survival needs, as is every animal species; but the human, as contrasted with lower animal forms, is more complex and must rely more on learned and adaptive behavior than on instinctive or innate predispositions. We are all familiar with signs of man's adjustments. He adjusts to his physical environment, to his culture and society, to his immediate family, and to his group of peers. Signs of these adjustments are everywhere: the Eskimo wears warm clothing and eats foods which are most accessible to him; the Dobuan adopts the rituals, mores, and taboos of his culture; the Frenchman speaks the language of his society; the upstate New Yorker tends to vote for the same political party as did his father; the college senior usually accepts a larger number of the values of his peer group than does the college freshman.

This process of adaptation could be explained by saying that the person has learned. In terms of fairly well-developed learning theories, studied by educators and psychologists over many years, we can say that man adapts to his environment by developing patterns of behavior which are reinforced or rewarded. As an act is performed and followed by reward, it tends to become fixed, tends to be repeated by the individual. The reinforcing rewards may be immediate and direct, as in the wearing of warm clothing. The comfort and protection of the clothing contributes to the well-being of the person and reinforces his behavior of wearing it; hence that behavior is repeated. On the other hand, the reward may be indirect or only anticipated. Why does a college senior tend to adopt the values of his peers? Why do people get on the bandwagon? The rewards for such conforming behavior often seem indirect rather than immediate. That behavior, however, is reinforced by the anticipation of acceptance and approval by one's peers. Such approval has likely followed similar conforming behavior in the past. So we can see that adaptive behavior is central to human existence, and we would explain such behavior by saying that it is learned or tends to be repeated because of direct or anticipated reward or reinforcement.

MAN PROVIDES ORDER TO HIS ENVIRONMENT

Human behavior is much more than adaptive. Man also adjusts the world to fit himself; he imposes order on nature. This is accomplished largely by means of categories or constructs and with the assistance of language.[2]

Categories

Our human senses are capable of discriminating seven million different colors; that is, if we could be shown all possible degrees of color brightness, hue, and saturation, we would be capable of distinguishing seven million different combinations. If a name were provided for each of these combinations, seven million names would be needed to describe color. Imagine trying to learn the names of seven million colors! It seems obvious that if it were necessary to treat each color possibility as a separate and equal entity, with a name for each, our understanding of color would break down. We could never learn the necessary vocabulary, remember it, or communicate with it.

Fortunately, we do not always have to consider the unique entities of this world as such. We are able to deal with these entities more efficiently by categorizing or combining them into sets. You are well aware of how this is done with color. Much of our thinking and our communication about color is possible with the terms red, orange, yellow, green, blue, indigo, violet; seven names rather than seven million. By subdividing these sets and using the concepts of brown, black, white, etc., a very specific conversation about the color of

2. This point is discussed in Hubert G. Alexander's book in Scott, Foresman's College Speech Series, *Meaning in Language.*

sweaters or paint for a dining room can be carried on with sixty or seventy terms.

There are three important points which must be emphasized concerning the categorizing activity of man. First, categorizing is a necessary process allowing us to understand and manipulate our environment. If we could not abstract and generalize, we could not reason efficiently or communicate at all, for we would be overwhelmed by the sheer number of sensations constantly bombarding us. This process permits us to reduce the complexity of our universe; it permits us to relate classes of events rather than individual events.

Aristotle emphasized that rhetoric is concerned with *classes* and not with individuals: "Rhetoric will consider not what seems probable to the individual—to Socrates or to Hippias—but what seems probable to a given class. . . ." Aristotle's discussion of classes of men can be used to illustrate the abstracting and generalizing process.[3] He characterizes *young men* by contrasting them with those of other ages: they have strong desires but are unsteady in their desires, they are trustful and sanguine, they have great hopes and live for the future, they are easily deceived, all their mistakes are on the side of intensity and excess. In this description Aristotle abstracts—he does not describe everything about every youth but rather focuses on those key criterial aspects of all youth as he sees them. In making the description, he generalizes—he extends his ideal description to cover all entities in the class (all young men). Exactness is lost in the process of abstraction and generalization, but this loss is necessary; we sacrifice precision and completeness in describing the individual case for the sake of general applicability.

Second, we must realize that our categories are man-made inventions, not discoveries; they exist in man rather than in nature. Again consider the color spectrum. The boundaries for *green* certainly do not exist on that continuum. Boundaries are established *arbitrarily* by man, and the single label *green* is applied to all shades falling between those boundaries. But though such boundaries are arbitrary, they are not set capriciously or without any direction. Our categories often are set up to satisfy some criteria. We usually choose and maintain categories that are able to stand up to pragmatic tests, that are usable and useful. Other standards, inherent in our make-up, may also be imposed. Note that the boundaries on the color spectrum for the seven labels mentioned above are approximately equally spaced along the color continuum (as measured in angstrom units). A desire for equivalence, parallelism, and completeness seems to influence the invention of many categories.

3. An excellent source on abstracting and generalizing is Harry L. Weinberg, *Levels of Knowing and Existence* (New York: Harper & Brothers, 1959), especially Chapter 4.

Third, while categories can be formed which reflect our reaction to physical objects or sensations resulting from external influence, not all categories refer to physical objects or events; they may also be formed for nonobservable or even hypothetical objects. Just as we form categories for the physical properties of color, so can we form categories which contain sets of feelings or values or internal fractional responses. To a large body of events and feelings we attach the labels *just* or *fair*. To even larger bodies we attach the labels *good* or *bad*. These categories represent feelings and values just as *green* and *hard* reflect physical properties.

Language

Categories provide boundaries for grouping our experiences; they are fences which corral sets of experience. One of the primary functions of language is to assign labels or names to these groupings or sets.[4] The processes of categorizing and labeling are interdependent. Categorizing establishes boundaries, while labeling establishes names. But labeling also involves processes of generalization and abstraction. A language label applies not so much to the total of the individual entities in the set as it applies to real or imagined properties of those entities. Thus, it is a generalization and abstraction of that set. The important common elements in the set are combined and narrowed, and it is this narrowed "meaning" of the category to which the label applies. Consider how the word *bottle* stimulates not a recollection of every bottle we have ever seen but rather a sense of the generalized and abstract criterial meanings we have come to attach to that word.

Man tends to give labels to all the different categories he discriminates, and, in turn, he discriminates among the different categories for which he has labels. Anthropologist Franz Boas points out, for example, that the Eskimo discriminates among many different categories for snow and ice and has dozens of labels for their various conditions. Fine shades of difference in the condition of ice and snow are extremely important to the Eskimo, and the ability to discriminate among them is more necessary to him than it is, for example, to the typical Illinoisan. All this again emphasizes how man adapts to his environment and, at the same time, imposes an order upon it so that he can better understand and control his own existence.

The labels applied to our categories provide a code with which we can manipulate symbolically the groupings into which we have

4. Important materials on the categorizing process can be found in Jerome S. Bruner, Jacqueline J. Goodnow, and George A. Austin, *A Study of Thinking* (New York: John Wiley & Sons, Inc., 1956). See Chapters 1, 2, and 3.

analyzed our universe. A person can manipulate the physical world by means of language. For example, if one is trapped in a burning building, it is not necessary to race about and try all potential escape routes solely by trial and error; it is possible to take that trip symbolically. One can stand and think through a particular escape route to its possible consequences. In this manner, language mediates between a man and his physical world.

Language also mediates between man and man. By means of a labeling code, one can communicate with his fellow man. We can transmit the symbol *green* and hope that, because of the common cultural environment in which we acquired that label, *green* will call up in our listener a set of reactions essentially similar to those we experience in response to that symbol. The overt and covert reactions we experience when confronted with a symbol are probably the best definition of the "meaning" that symbol has for us.

The likelihood that the speaker and listener will have essentially similar reactions is greater for the symbol *green* than it is for the symbol *freedom*. The sensations which produce a response of *green* can be measured along a single continuum with scientific instrumentation. We could stabilize our judgments on that label with relatively high reliability if we were willing to invest the effort required; that is, we could obtain fairly good agreement in setting the boundaries of *green* along the color spectrum. But the symbol *freedom* is a broader and higher level abstraction. As contrasted with the boundaries for *green*, the boundaries for the category or set delineating responses we label *freedom* are not nearly so clear. We are not at all sure that *freedom* is a single-dimensional concept. It might be viewed along many dimensions and would then require many sets of boundaries. And the continua are not so clear as is the wave length of reflected light.

It is important here that we see language as a means whereby we arbitrarily assign labels to categories we have established so that we may manipulate those categories of objects, processes, etc., rather than deal with infinite individual entities. We employ symbols to think about events and to communicate about events. Our overt and covert responses to a symbol define operationally the "meaning" we ascribe to it.

Reasoning

Psychologist Norman Munn has defined reasoning as the sequential arousal and manipulation of language symbols. Man reasons by associating the labels he has applied to categories of experience. The labels themselves serve to identify generalizations and abstractions of that experience. The association of these symbols allows for inference, the process by which a person derives new propositions or conclusions from previously established propositions and data.

Stephen Toulmin, in *The Uses of Argument*, presents his layout of this inferential process.[5] According to Toulmin's description, we infer from *evidence*, or data, to a *conclusion*, or claim, by means of the connector of a *warrant*, or general proposition.

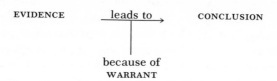

Toulmin suggests that the warrant itself may be given support, called *backing*, and that the conclusion might still not follow if countered by other objections, called *rebuttal*. He also recognizes the weakness of absolutism and includes a *qualifier* before the conclusion. His full model for an argument (or line of reasoning) is represented by the following diagram:

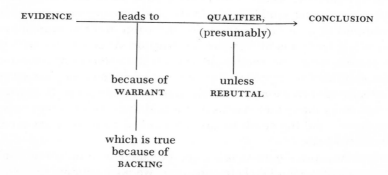

In terms of our previous discussion, Toulmin's warrant represents a relatively abstract generalization one has already arrived at or accepted, and evidence represents a fairly specific item of information. The inferential process attempts to subsume the specific evidence under the generalization of the warrant. Once this is done, an association is drawn between the evidence and other particulars (including the conclusion) also subsumed under the warrant. This association of particulars through the processes of categorizing and generalizing is the essence of inference.

5. Stephen Toulmin, *The Uses of Argument* (Cambridge: Cambridge University Press, 1958). Chapter 3, "The Layout of Arguments," covers in detail the material sketched here.

An example used by Toulmin illustrates the procedure by which a person might draw the inference that Harry is a British subject from the knowledge that Harry was born in Bermuda. The inference is laid out as follows:

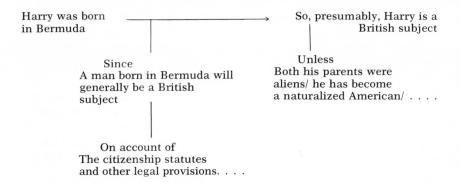

Harry was born in Bermuda ————————————→ So, presumably, Harry is a British subject

Since
A man born in Bermuda will generally be a British subject

Unless
Both his parents were aliens/ he has become a naturalized American/ . . . .

On account of
The citizenship statutes and other legal provisions. . . .

Toulmin's system, like the syllogistic system of Aristotle discussed in Chapter 1, is helpful for analyzing the process of human inference. There have been numerous attempts to apply both of these systems to speech manuscripts to assist in the analysis of argument; but it seems likely that the systems are most useful in analysis of the inferential process of a potential speaker prior to the speaking occasion and of a listener during the speaking occasion. That is, we may best use them to focus upon the person of the speaker or listener rather than upon a speech manuscript, because so many elements in the inferential process (e.g., unstated assumptions, value judgments) are omitted from the message communicated and must be discovered within the communicator or within his audience. This is the point of the distinction mentioned earlier between the syllogism and the rhetorical enthymeme: the syllogism, representing formal logic, is complete within itself; the enthymeme, representing rhetorical discourse such as persuasion, depends for its completion upon value judgments and unstated assumptions that are presumably shared by speaker and listener.

This is not the place to go into detail concerning technical aspects of logic, nor is it necessary to do so, but two myths regarding man's rational nature should be corrected before proceeding further. The first is a belief that logical thinking will automatically lead to truth, and the second is the supposition that there exists some conflict between our logical and our emotional natures.

On the first point, it should be emphasized that logical thought serves primarily to make our thinking consistent and cannot guarantee the "truth" of our conclusions. Given certain premises, we find what sorts of conclusions can and cannot follow; but we are told little about the truth of the premises or the basic beliefs from which we start. A man's thinking may be rigorously logical, but if his initial grounds are false, his inferences and conclusions will also be false. The delusions of some mentally ill persons are entirely consistent with one another and fit the tests of sound logical reasoning. They are well-reasoning persons even if not rational. Their problem is a lack of contact with reality and not a faulty manipulation of reality. Their categories for reasoning do not accurately represent the ranges of experience they are supposed to generalize.

The second point, involving emotion and reason, has long been a source of difficulty to writers on persuasion. Some have written of emotion and reason as distinct and opposed elements; as a speech contains more of one, it contains less of the other. Occasionally a distinction has been drawn between appeals to emotion and appeals to reason. These views are likely to be extremely misleading.

The better position is that emotion and reason are always conjoined in any communicative act. Writing on cognitive theory, Martin Scheerer maintains:

> In principle, then, behavior may be conceptualized as being embedded in a cognitive-emotional-motivational matrix in which no true separation is possible. No matter how we slice behavior, the ingredients of motivation-emotion-cognition are present in one order or another. As Adams succinctly expressed it, "For there is a conative or dynamic component in our most disinterested, scientific, and objective cognition, or we would not make the observation. There is likewise a cognitive component in our blindest lust or rage, or their expressions would not have even the minimum of direction that they seem invariably to have."[6]

From this point of view, we see that no communication can fail to appeal to emotion, to touch upon our affective system. At the same time, no communication received can fail to involve the arousal and manipulation of symbols, which is our understanding of the process of reasoning.

Here, again, the problem in part is that long-standing need of man to have his actions be explainable, reasonable, rational. This need causes us to rationalize frequently, to invent plausible reasons if we cannot find probable reasons. For example: "I do have a test

6. Martin Scheerer, "Cognitive Theory," in *Handbook of Social Psychology,* ed. Gardner Lindzey (Cambridge: Addison-Wesley Publishing Company, Inc., 1954), I, p. 123.

tomorrow, but the movie would be relaxing, and besides, if I don't know it now, I never will."

Not only are emotional responses and reasoning processes conjoint; we have some evidence that they are positively correlated. Psychologists Hebb and Thompson report:

> Evidence from species comparison suggests that emotional susceptibility increases with intellectual capacity. Man is the most emotional as well as the most rational animal. . . .
>
> Such phylogenetic and ontogenetic correlations between increasing intellect and increasing emotionality would suggest that thought and emotion are intimately, essentially related. There must be doubt concerning any treatment of emotion as a state or process independent of intellectual processes, and having a separate seat in the nervous system.[7]

The point is that, between species and within species, emotion and reasoning are positively related. From rat to dog to chimpanzee to man (moron) to man (genius), intellectual capacity and emotional capacity increase steadily, and they increase together.

This finding seems to conflict not only with the need to appear rational but also with many of our observations of everyday life. It is not often that we observe an intelligent man showing extreme overt emotional reaction. How is this fact to be explained if we do not assume a dichotomy between reason and emotion? The sounder explanation is that man can use his intelligence to avoid those situations in which his responses would be extremely emotional. The more intelligent man is more capable of that avoidance. But when placed in the situation without choice, the emotional behavior of the intelligent man will be more variable and more intense. We may summarize these observations by saying that the reasoning process involves the sequential arousal and manipulation of mediating language symbols, that this capacity for reasoning is positively correlated with emotional sensitivity, and that while reason and emotion (like any other language categories) may be considered separately in the abstract, they are necessarily conjoined in any concrete persuasive speaking occasion.

A final comment should be made concerning the reasoning process. From studies of decision making and from the theory of games, we find that there are different patterns of reasoning; not every man approaches a given problem in the same way. In terms of the Toulmin model, it is likely that some persons focus more on the

7. D. O. Hebb and W. R. Thompson, "The Social Significance of Animal Studies," in *Handbook of Social Psychology*, pp. 553–555.

evidence than they do on the warrant; their most careful checks are applied to evidence. Others are more concerned with general principles, focusing more upon warrants. Some are keen to sense possible rebuttal; others appear oblivious to these possibilities. And there are other patterns for manipulating symbols so as to arrive at new understandings. For example, Bruner, Goodnow, and Austin in *A Study of Thinking* describe such patterns as simultaneous scanning, successive scanning, conservative focusing, and focus gambling.[8] In solving a problem, one person may attempt to see the overall picture: he engages in simultaneous scanning. Another may focus upon and vary one element of his perception at a time: he is engaging in conservative focusing behavior. There is not much new that we can say now about these patterns. Much research work needs to be done on patterns of reasoning in persuasive speaking settings.

What must be said now about man's logical reasoning process is, first, that it employs symbols as we have discussed them; second, that it leads to internal consistency but not necessarily to truth; and, finally, that it is itself motivated behavior rather than being divorced from the emotions.

Beliefs and attitudes

We have been discussing the manner in which man categorizes his sensations and applies labels so that he may think and talk about sets of experience by means of symbols. Our examples have had to do mainly with the labeling functions of symbols. These examples have demonstrated how we establish boundaries for a category and then apply a label. But labels can serve to show relationships as well as to define and delimit. Such terms as *certain, impossible, good, bad* show relationship. An event we label as *certain* would, from our view, be more likely to occur than would an event we label *uncertain*. An event we label *good* would, from our view, be more desirable and would serve as greater reward than an event we label *bad*. As with our other symbols, these labels are applied to our responses and are individual; thus, what one man labels *good*, another might call *bad*.

Most people interested in social psychology consider beliefs and attitudes to be central to the study of human behavior. Our position here is that beliefs and affects are learned responses, are meanings applied to our concepts, and are at the heart of the persuasive speaking process. Much of our discussion of persuasive speaking will focus on belief and attitude. (The views of Fishbein, mentioned in Chapter 1,

8. Bruner, op. cit. See Chapters 4–8.

will be helpful here.) Like our other symbols, labels bearing on belief and attitude are employed by man to aid in bringing order and coherence to his adjustment to reality.

By *belief*, we mean that dimension of meaning which labels the *probableness* of an event.[9] "It will rain tomorrow" is a proposition with an associated degree of probability ranging from 0 (impossible) to 1 (certain). Our guess of the probability of that event might be .30 or .50 or perhaps .75. However finely we set the gradations along this probability continuum, each position represents a category into which we can fit our event. The category we employ adds the dimension of belief or probableness to our meaning for the proposition.

"Candidate X will be elected," "A business recession is likely next year," "Increased study time will improve grades for the average student" — all are propositions to which any of us would very likely ascribe some degree of probability. We would fit each of these propositions into a category of belief. The purpose of a persuasive speech often is to shift a person's belief: to change the degree of probability he ascribes to a proposition, or to change the category of belief to which he assigns the proposition.

Attitude is an additional dimension of meaning. Attitude is the positive or negative *feeling, affect,* or *evaluation* we associate with an object or event. We may view attitudes as we did beliefs — as points along a continuum — but there is some advantage to looking at attitudes as points along *two* continua: 0 to 1 on a *positive affect* dimension, and 0 to 1 on a *negative affect* dimension.

One person may evaluate candidate X very highly. He may categorize X as .85 along the positive dimension and 0 on the negative dimension. This means he has very positive, favorable feelings toward X and no negative feelings. Another person may evaluate X as .85 on the positive dimension and .25 on the negative dimension. This would mean that he generally has strong positive feelings about X but that he also has some negative associations. A third person may view candidate X as 0 or .10 on both dimensions, indicating little association, positive or negative, with X. Another may categorize X as .60 positive and .60 negative. He would experience ambivalent reactions to X. He would have "mixed emotions."

To distinguish these two dimensions of attitude is important. On most concepts considered in persuasive speaking situations, such as

9. For a view of different types of beliefs, the reader may wish to read the text of the speech "Images of the Consumer's Changing Mind On and Off Madison Avenue," by Milton Rokeach, included in *The Speaker's Resource Book,* ed. Carroll C. Arnold, Douglas Ehninger, and John C. Gerber (Glenview, Ill.: Scott, Foresman and Company, 1966), pp. 115–121. This book contains a number of speech texts which could be used for analysis.

"mercy killing," "federal government power," and all "candidates X," we probably have some degree of *both* positive and negative feeling or affect. Rarely do attitudes lie along a single continuum running *from* negative *to* positive.

Designations of attitude can be regarded as labels assigned to categories of experience, as can expressions of belief. Attitude is an important dimension of the meaning which any object or event has for us; therefore, a shift in attitude often represents an end or purpose of persuasive speaking. We will discuss changes in belief and attitude at greater length in the next chapter.

Values

The final topic in our discussion of the ways in which man orders his existence is that of *values*. Our systems of values represent higher level abstractions and more general categories than those discussed thus far. Beliefs and attitudes may be seen as combining to form our systems of values. These systems are learned and determine our style of life.

Eduard Spranger, a German scholar, developed a theory of human behavior in which he maintained that there are six primary types of man, labeling these types according to their dominant values.[10] Spranger agrees that any person certainly has more than one set of values influencing his behavior, but he argues that any man will have one predominant value system. Spranger lists six major value types as follows:

Theoretical	values pursuit of and discovery of truth, the "intellectual" life.
Economic	values that which is useful, practical.
Aesthetic	values form, harmony, and beauty.
Social	values love, sympathy, warmth, and sensitivity in relationships with people.
Political	values competition, influence, personal power.
Religious	values unity, wholeness, a sense of purpose above man.

Although it is probably impossible to draw up a specific list of the value systems held by all men, Spranger's list serves to clarify what is meant by a "value system" and to indicate the potential influence of these systems in persuasive speaking, from the point of view of both speaker and listener.

10. Eduard Spranger, *Types of Men*, trans. P. Prigors from the 5th German edition (Haale [Saale]: M. Niemeyer, 1928).

Psychiatrist Jurgen Ruesch, in *Communication: The Social Matrix of Psychiatry*, advances the view that American values show certain emphases: Puritan and pioneer morality; Equality; Sociality; Success; Change.[11] One can see some similarities between this system and that of Spranger, although the basic categorization and labeling do differ.

Our lives are dominated by systems of value. An "economic" man will want to speak and hear about economic topics and propositions. He will be more sensitive and responsive to economic issues. His interpretation of almost any topic will bear the economic stamp. Value systems cannot be turned on or off at will; a strong value system will pervade an individual's behavior.

In this section, we have discussed many means used by man to provide order to his existence: categories, language, reasoning, beliefs, attitudes, and values. Since none of them is innate or inherited, it follows that all these devices and procedures are learned. They are learned through direct experience, by trial and error behavior, part of which is reinforced and becomes fixed. They are also learned from the experience of others as that experience is observed by us or related to us. This vicarious experience is especially important because so much of what we feel and so many of our patterns of behavior are products of our accepting a voice of authority. In childhood we are often rewarded for complying with the wishes and patterns of authority figures. It is little wonder that in our adult years we find it difficult to question authority.

MAN'S BEHAVIOR IS MOTIVATED

Thus far we have emphasized that man adapts to reality as he sees it, that he provides order to it by categorizing and by assigning labels to his categories so that he can manipulate reality symbolically, and that he learns beliefs, attitudes, and values which add further meaning to his categories. As we look further at man in his environment, we see that he often seems impelled to action. The living human, in fact, is never entirely at rest. Unfortunately, human motivation is one of those complex subjects about which we do not have as many answers as we should like; but certain basic principles of human motivation will help us understand this process and place it in proper context when discussing persuasive speaking. In particular, we

11. Jurgen Ruesch and Gregory Bateson, *Communication: The Social Matrix of Psychiatry* (New York: W. W. Norton and Company, Inc., 1951). See Chapter 4, "Communication and American Values."

will want to consider how motives energize and provide direction for behavior.

A number of psychologists have divided this topic into *primary motives* and *secondary motives,* a rather useful and usable classification of human striving. *Primary motives* are taken to cover those basic physiological needs which must be satisfied if the life of the individual and his species is to continue. *Secondary motives* are the learned, social needs.

Somewhat more detailed and helpful is the general theory of motivation developed by A. H. Maslow.[12] He lists five basic needs, rank-ordered according to their prepotency: Physiological, Safety, Belongingness and Love, Esteem, Self-actualization. The physiological needs are the demands of the individual for food, water, procreation, and homeostasis. These needs are basic to life and must be satisfied *first.* Safety needs are on a higher level. Man desires an orderly, smoothly functioning world in which sudden, unexpected, and potentially dangerous events do not occur often. He wants to feel settled and at ease rather than threatened.

The belongingness and love needs reflect man's social nature. Man desires to be loved by family and friends. He wants to belong, to be "in." On the next level are the esteem needs. Man likes to have self-esteem, self-respect, a reasonably high evaluation of himself, and he desires the esteem and respect of others. He seeks status; he likes to be recognized and appreciated.

The highest level need is self-actualization or self-fulfillment. We know of persons — artists, writers, political leaders — who seem to have all the other needs satisfied and yet are still motivated to action. Maslow would call this behavior the product of self-actualization; a man must be what he can be.

Maslow's theory holds that these needs display a hierarchy of prepotency. In other words, the physiological needs come first. Unless satisfied to a moderate degree, all activity will be directed toward physiological needs. If the physiological needs are reasonably well satisfied, then the higher level needs will serve as motivators. Maslow realizes, of course, that this hierarchy is not rigid and that the lower level needs do not require complete satisfaction before the higher level needs begin to influence activity. But one should not look for much evidence of self-actualization behavior unless the lower level needs appear to be fairly well met. Maslow's categorization of needs and the concept of prepotency will be helpful in reaching a better understanding of the persuasive process.

12. A. H. Maslow, *Motivation and Personality* (New York: Harper & Brothers, 1954.) Primarily Chapter 5, "A Theory of Human Motivation."

Another helpful concept is that of the functional autonomy of motives. This principle, developed by Gordon Allport,[13] maintains that behaviors and desires which are learned to satisfy more basic needs may eventually become motivators themselves, even in the absence of the more basic and originally associated need. For example, we all had a grandfather who worked hard to provide food and shelter for his family in difficult times. Even after he had provided the necessities of life and all were comfortable, he continued to work hard. Strenuous effort had become a part of him, and he was driven to it for itself alone long after the original need had been satisfied. We can see how the values mentioned earlier could become functionally autonomous and serve as motivators of behavior.

For the most part these motivations are helpful; they provide the drive and help shape the direction of our behavior. Motivations, however, are a mixed blessing. The blocking of a goal, coupled with the continuance of a drive, can lead to frustration. Frustration in turn can lead to aggression or to even less adaptive behavior, such as flight tendencies, negativism, defeatism, and even withdrawal from reality.

MAN'S BEHAVIOR IS CHECKED AND LIMITED

The ends man strives for cannot always be achieved. Natural endowments and learned abilities set definite limitations on behavior. One cannot see, hear, or smell those stimuli which fall outside his sensory thresholds. One cannot think beyond his own intellectual capacity or work beyond his physical limitations. A deafened Beethoven composed great music, but a congenitally deaf Beethoven likely could not have.

Just as one's actions are checked by limitations within his person, so are they further directed and checked from without. Some of the influences of physical environment and of society upon the individual were mentioned earlier when we discussed man's adaptive behavior. Clothing and vocabulary were examples. A person may be driven from within to seek the esteem of others but may be directed by them in the behaviors by which he seeks it. As we have already noted, a number of psychological studies have dramatized man's tendency to conform. One will often go along with the crowd or get on the bandwagon even when his private personal judgment is at variance with that of "the crowd."

13. Gordon W. Allport, "The Functional Autonomy of Motives," *American Journal of Psychology*, L (1937), 141–156.

Potential behavior is also checked by habit. Our habits are something like our categories; they are ways of generalizing and abstracting experience. When we learn a complex task such as driving a car or doing a new dance step, we must first concentrate all our attentions on the activity. We focus as much as possible on the specific task and are acutely aware of each individual substep of the process. As we learn, the complex series of interrelated steps blend together; we are able to perform the entire task without consciously focusing upon it alone. We can pay more attention to the road and outside events without thinking about individual acts of shifting gears or applying brakes. We can converse with our dance partner (in dance forms where proximity is possible) or focus on other dancers without concentrating on what our left foot is doing at the moment. In short, we have developed habits.

Habituated behavior allows us to perform complex tasks while engaged in additional activities. It allows us to be broader in the scope of our behavior and to apply ourselves to higher levels of abstract thought. At the same time, as they become strong, habits do much to regulate our potential behavior. For instance, accuracy of speech articulation is largely habitual. While we "monitored" or listened closely to our own articulation when we learned to speak as children, we quickly developed language habits that allowed us to drop that conscious and active monitoring. If the articulation habits we formed were socially desirable, all is well; but if those learned habits of speech do not now fit the expectations of the society in which we live, then relearning is necessary. In trying to learn new habits of articulation, we would become painfully aware of the way in which habit can limit behavior. When the new behaviors we are attempting to learn run counter to our fixed habits, that new learning is especially difficult.

Earlier we discussed the central role played in human behavior by belief and attitude structures and by systems of values. These predisposing factors, when they are learned and have our commitment, serve not only to guide our behavior but also to constrain our activity.

In this chapter we have described the physical, social, ideational, and individual world as confronting man with a reality that is changing and developing in size and complexity. We described man as a creature with remarkable facility to adapt and to provide order to this changing environment. He achieves order largely by categorizing, generalizing, and abstracting his experience and then manipulating it by means of language and thought processes.

To promote order, man learns belief, attitude, and value systems. He comes upon these systems through his own experience, through observing the experience of others, and through accepting authority. As his behavior, based on these systems, is rewarded—directly or by expectation—that behavior is learned and becomes habitual.

Added to this, human behavior is motivated—stimulated to activity and directed to goals. If frustrated or blocked, an individual can react with a number of regressive and withdrawal behavior patterns. Even when not blocked, motivated behavior is restricted and channeled by individual ability and aptitude limitations, by habits, and by social and physical environment.

Out of such dynamic and complex interaction of forces and processes, a man comes to propositions or ends which involve others or for which he requires the assistance of others. On these occasions he may turn to persuasive speaking as the means to effect his ends. Moreover, his auditors come to the speaking situation with their own backgrounds of experience and their own categories, attitudes, beliefs, motives, and habits of thought and behavior. The forces and processes presented here are the antecedents to their interaction—to persuasive speaking.

3.

THE OCCASION AND END

OF PERSUASIVE SPEAKING

Our United States Ambassador to the United Nations urges the Security Council to vote for a censure of another nation. A member of middle-management urges adoption of a new production plan. A little boy pleads with his mother for another treat. From the political hustings to the family kitchen, persuasive speaking is all about us. Because of the demands for mutual rapport and involvement, it could be argued that two humans can achieve their closest intellectual contact in a persuasive speaking situation.

This chapter and the next will consider the essential features of the process through which this primary form of human interaction occurs. We regard persuasive speaking as a dynamic sequence of events which are intimately interrelated; that is, we view it as a *process*,[1] a dynamic activity rather than a static event. In an anthology of speeches we could read the manuscript of a persuasive speech given by Daniel Webster over a hundred years ago or of a speech given more recently by Adlai Stevenson; but in both cases we would be viewing only a part of the "history" of a persuasive speaking event. We would not be viewing the activity itself, for persuasive speaking exists only in those moments when it is occurring. By studying only the "history" or the "traces" of a persuasive speaking occurrence, we can be easily misled into viewing it as a static event. The complexities of the activity are then obscured, and the resulting analysis may tend to be oversimplified and misleading. As an anti-

1. This point is discussed in Theodore Clevenger, Jr., and Jack Matthews' book in Scott, Foresman's College Speech Series, *The Speech Communication Process.*

dote to this tendency, in this chapter we will consider the *occasion* of persuasive speaking and the *end* sought through persuasive speaking.

THE OCCASION OF PERSUASIVE SPEAKING

The persuasive speaking occasion or situation typically is considered to involve a persuader, a persuadee, and a setting. These may be regarded as the primary elements of the activity.

Persuader

The persuader usually has the greatest immediate stake in the activity, for he is the person who is consciously attempting to influence another. He initiates the activity, and the consequences of the act usually are considered in terms of his ends or in terms of the proposition he advances.

We err often, however, in thinking of the persuader as a single person. The persuader may just as well be multiple—even so multiple as to lose "personness." Our United Nations representatives, for instance, are speaking for our nation. It is as if our country were the person of the persuader and the particular representative merely the spokesman or go-between. Certainly in this case it is the image of the government involved that is most persuasive and not primarily the image of the specific spokesman of the moment.

Persuadee

The persuadee is the person to whom the persuasive speech is directed. It is influence on his behavior which is sought. As with the persuader, the size of the group involved may become so large that, in effect, an entire nation is the object of the message.

In the preceding chapter, we considered the persuader's view of reality and examined the influences affecting the propositions he decides to advocate. It should be clear that a persuadee meets reality in a similar manner, although the categories, the associated meanings, and the strategies for manipulating categories will differ for any two men. A persuader and a persuadee are quite alike as men confronting reality and yet are different in the roles they play in a persuasive speaking situation.

Changing roles of persuader and persuadee

While the designations of persuader and persuadee are essential for analysis, we must keep in mind that in the persuasive speaking act these roles are neither mutually exclusive nor static. In conversation and group discussion, the roles often are interchanged, and the persuader of one moment becomes the persuadee of the next. And even in a public speaking setting, while one acts as persuader, he may be influenced by the reactions of his audience and therefore be simultaneously persuader (insofar as we consider what he says and does in the speech) and persuadee (insofar as we consider how audience reactions influence him).

Let us consider more fully how a single individual may play these roles simultaneously. Communication theorists write about feedback, which is the reception of stimuli that allow for correction and modification of behavior. The thermostat is a feedback device which serves to control temperature in a building: when the temperature falls to a certain level, the furnace is activated; when the temperature rises to a certain level, the furnace is turned off. This regulating mechanism maintains a desired range of temperature by receiving messages and then making adjustments to maintain this temperature range. The human organism contains numerous feedback mechanisms which serve as homeostatic devices. They keep body temperature, blood sugar level, and many other factors within desired ranges.

In the communication act, the audience provides feedback cues to which the speaker may adjust. The facial expressions of some audience members may reveal puzzlement, and the speaker may react by going back over his point with additional clarifying materials. Or the audience may appear bored, and the speaker may react by interjecting some humorous material. When an audience in Liverpool reacted negatively by heckling a point in his speech, Henry Ward Beecher is reported to have said, "All I ask is simply fair play." Fair play apparently was a value embraced by most in his audience, for it is reported that he had no further interruptions for the next few minutes. Beecher's impromptu statement is an example of successful adaptation to feedback from the audience. When speaking in favor of black nationalism to a college audience, the then Black Muslim leader Malcolm X sensed a negative reaction by his audience to his rate and intensity of delivery. He attempted to adjust to this feedback by saying, "I'm sorry to be talking so fast, but I haven't much time, and I do have a lot to say." If he hopes to be effective, any persuader must be sensitive to such audience cues, must be able to interpret them accurately, and must be able to react to them in ways which increase his persuasive appeal. But in every act of adapting to audience feedback, the speaker is in effect allowing the audience to modify certain aspects of his own behavior. From these examples of feedback, we can see how an audience may influence a speaker even as the speaker influences the audience.

There is yet a deeper level at which this reciprocal influence of persuader and persuadee may be noted. One view of leadership could be termed the "followership" theory of leadership. This view would suggest that a leader does not lead in the sense that we usually consider it but rather "follows" the group or audience; he accurately assesses the view of the group and then serves as a spokesman for it. The people *appear* to follow him because he "gives them what they want." Is this type of speaker in actuality a persuader or is he a persuadee? Some politicians have been accused of "kite flying": they tentatively advance a number of issues and look for audience reaction; then they take up as "causes" those issues which get a sympathetic reaction from their audience. For instance, a politician may advance views on public housing and on communism, then drop housing and take up the "cause" of anticommunism because it appears to be more salient for his audience. Is this man leading his audience or following it? Or is he leading part of his audience by following another part? Although he gives strong speeches and appears to be a vigorous advocate, is he more truly playing the role of persuader or of persuadee?

While our major concern is with the effects of speaker upon listener, we must not be unaware of the effects of an audience upon a speaker. These examples serve to show that the designations *persuader* and *persuadee* are not so easily applied when we view persuasive speaking as a process. An individual is rarely, if ever, exclusively one or the other.

Nevertheless, when discussed with proper qualification and in the proper context, the designations of persuader and persuadee *roles* can be helpful. An important distinction between them can be made in terms of the position taken toward the specific proposition advanced in the persuasive speech. In any persuasive speaking situation, the positions taken by persuader and persuadee toward the proposition will differ, at least initially. The persuader will have a fairly well-settled position on the proposition. As explained in the last chapter, he has a set of beliefs and affects about the proposition which combine to represent his viewpoint. While this view may be modified as he speaks, it is a definite and compelling position as he begins to speak. The persuadee, on the other hand, may begin with any one of a number of possible positions on the proposition. He might be essentially favorable toward the proposition, and this tendency could range from moderate interest to enthusiastic support. Or he might be unfavorable. He might be ambivalent toward the proposition, with both positive and negative feelings, and these feelings may be somewhat balanced. The persuadee could be indifferent toward the proposal. He might be aware of it but uncommitted, without strong feelings on either side. Or he might be uninformed, unaware of any controversy on the point at issue.[2]

These differences in initial position toward a proposition are a necessary condition for the persuasive speaking situation and provide a means for distinguishing persuader from persuadee. From this view we can see that for the majority of his audience our kite-flying politician is not giving a persuasive speech after all, for there is no difference between his position and the predominate view of his audience. He is trying to change their attitudes, certainly – but just towards a more favorable view of himself. It seems that many who have criticized rhetoric throughout the ages have in reality been damning this type of thing – this electioneering. When we draw a distinction between audience flattery and influence in the terms presented here, we can direct some of the criticism to its proper concern, and that concern is not with the most respected goals of persuasive speaking. This is not to say that speeches of flattery are necessarily bad or undesirable. After all, a good deal of our conversation occurs with friends with whom we are in complete agreement. The point to be made here is that both flattery and social conversation, even when purposefully influential in modifying beliefs and behavior, should be considered as distinct from persuasive speaking.

Setting

The third element in the persuasive speaking occasion is the setting. Setting covers all aspects of the situation other than persuader and persuadee. It includes such factors as time, place, physical environment, and psychological atmosphere. Even with the same participants, differences in setting can change the persuasive activity.

It is not without purpose that the evangelist uses music and crowd participation in his service. Demagogues do not seek assembled throngs as audiences for the sole purpose of spreading their messages efficiently; they realize the effects of a "mass." Much has been written about audience polarization and social facilitation. *Polarization* is the common focusing of attention upon the same stimulus – the all-to-one relation in which the individuals of the audience respond to the single object of attention, the speaker. *Social facilitation* refers to the effect of the members of an audience upon one another because of their physical proximity. When a few individuals begin to applaud, others in the audience tend to join in the applause. The point is that in a large group, all behavior is magnified and the focus of our concern is drawn more to factors outside our

2. This point is discussed in Paul D. Holtzman's book in Scott, Foresman's College Speech Series, *The Psychology of Speakers' Audiences.*

own person. In a sense, then, we can lose a measure of control-by-self in that setting. Since the focus is drawn to grosser behavior by the very size of the setting, we can well expect less subtle behavior. Any persuader seeking major and easily observable changes in behavior will give careful consideration to factors in the setting. In the face of the human instinct toward self-preservation, it is little wonder that persuaders who ask us to lay down our lives employ uniforms and robes, flags and medals, and music—all centering around large-group activity.

There would seem to be two prerequisites for any situation if the persuasive process is to occur. These are (1) a proximity of persuader and persuadee and (2) the transmission of language symbols.

The persuader and persuadee must be physically and psychologically proximate. You might say that this is obvious, for the persuadee certainly must be able to hear the persuader's voice; but in addition to being able to hear, the persuadee must be willing to listen, which involves the element of psychological proximity. This is also obvious. But too many writers on persuasion assume that since these conditions are obviously necessary, they will necessarily occur. A substantial body of research on mass media communication seems to indicate that this proximity does not occur so routinely. In fact, mass media seem to have little influence on partisans for this very reason. A person with a commitment on a social issue usually reads, watches, and speaks with sources that argue *for* his view and generally has little contact with sources that argue *against* it. Republicans listen to Republicans and Democrats listen to Democrats. Very few persons who vote against a political candidate ever listen to or read very much of what he says, or writes, or endorses about political issues.

The difficulty of persuading those with extreme positions on any issue is discussed by Sherif and Hovland:

> Here, the problem of changing the individual's position through communication is exceedingly difficult. Even a communication designed to present a moderate point of view may be regarded by the recipient with an extremely "pro" stand as being somewhat "con" in its approach. The advocated position falls squarely within his latitude of rejection and, far from convincing him, the communication is more likely to reinforce his own entrenched stand.[3]

Books subtitled "How to Succeed in 10 Easy Lessons" usually advise us on how to handle a hostile audience, but they rarely tell us

3. Sherif and Hovland, op. cit., pp. 194–195.

where to find one. Finding "hostiles" usually is easy, but finding "hostiles" who will comprise an audience, in the sense of being psychologically proximate with the speaker, is another matter. In large measure, *hostile audience* is a contradiction in terms.

The fact is that in our society, a great deal of persuasion that may be desired, and even desirable, is impossible because the condition of proximity cannot be met. It takes two to tango. It also takes two for a persuasive speaking setting. Human contact is difficult enough to achieve, but the bases for human interaction are even more limited. We must remember that every person is a "subject" to himself but an "object" to everyone else. And as Alexander Pope wrote, our judgments are like our watches: no two go just alike, yet each believes his own. One must not confuse an ineffective persuasive attempt with a situation which cannot even be considered a persuasive setting because of the absence of proximity between persuader and persuadee. If we confuse these two situations by viewing them as alike, we shall lose much of the sharpness of our analysis of persuasive speaking.

The second prerequisite for a persuasive speaking setting is the transmission of verbal symbols. We commented in the last chapter on the nature of symbols and on the fact that in communication the connecting link between individuals is the verbal symbol. One person speaks a word or sentence with some type of inflection, while assuming a certain posture, with a certain facial expression, and accompanied perhaps by a pattern of gestures. This person is sending out numerous visible and audible cues that reveal his ideas, feelings, beliefs, desires, and intentions. Each of these cues reveals something about the speaker. At times some cues will conflict. When responding to the suggestion of a good-night kiss, the young lady may *say* "no," but with an inflection that carries her truer *feeling*, "maybe." A speaker's words may show strength, whereas his posture reveals weakness; the unsteady hand and the lack of eye contact may say more than the sentences spoken.

The "meaning" which the speaker transmits is carried not simply by his words but by everything he does, and the same is true of the "meaning" which the listener receives. The persuasive setting is always such that a speaker has only the ability to *transmit* a message, to send it out. Reception of the message depends upon the listener. A persuasive speaker cannot transfer meanings; he can only send out visible and audible cues. If his audience is psychologically proximate to him, those cues will arouse one set of associations and be interpreted in one way; but if his listeners are psychologically remote, their interpretation of the transmitted cues is likely to be quite different.

This, then, is the occasion of persuasive speaking. Although sometimes difficult to separate, its elements are a persuader, a persuadee, and a setting. In some ways, persuader and persuadee could better be considered as "roles" rather than as persons, both played simultaneously by a persuasive speaker and by his listener. The setting involves the factors of the persuasive speaking situation beyond the personalities involved. Proximity and the transmission of language symbols between participants are necessary or criterial conditions for a persuasive speaking situation.

THE END OF PERSUASIVE SPEAKING

The end or goal of persuasive speaking is influence. Persuasive speaking was defined earlier as that situation in which one is making a conscious effort to influence the behavior of another by the transmission of audible and visible symbolic cues. It is true that one may influence the behavior of unintended receivers by being overheard. Or one may even have his gestures or word patterns copied without any intentions on his part. These are conditions of influence, but they are not considered here as instances of persuasion. Enough has been said about language to show how arbitrary such a definition is. These side-effects could well be included in a definition of persuasive speaking influence, but such a definition would expand the scope of persuasive speaking to cover the whole of human interaction. While in some ways this might be justified, it tends to make our topic unmanageable. We have, therefore, limited our consideration to conscious and purposeful attempts at influence by speech.

Before proceeding further, we might do well to consider just how great is the potential influence of conscious and deliberate attempts to influence others through persuasive discourse. This is a question which is surrounded by misunderstandings arising from popular myths and fashionable anxieties. There are those who would have us experience all manner of fears as we contemplate the potential of persuasion in society. They caution us to beware of advertising, brainwashing, subliminal persuasion, and the world of 1984. However, the facts hardly support exaggerated fears of the powers of persuasion. We have already commented on the difficulties of achieving the proximity needed for persuasion even to be possible. Moreover, in most of the hundreds of studies on persuasion, we find that a single message has only a limited effect, and that effect diminishes with the passage of time. The persuadee tends to move back toward his original position. In their summary of the contribution of behavioral science research, Bernard Berelson and Gary Steiner have repeatedly been forced to emphasize the lack of evidence supporting the persuasive influence of mass media of communication, brainwashing, subliminal persuasion, and even of psychotherapy.[4] Commentators on the passing scene and popular writers must always have their fears. A moderate and relatively remote fear is exciting, and these writers, like advertisers, have a vested interest in what will sell.

But it would be wrong for us to accept an exaggerated fear of persuasive speaking. The evidence seems to indicate that the possible influence of a typical persuasive speech is limited in immediate effect, and even more limited if lasting effect is desired. A single persuasive speech is not likely to change basic value systems learned over a lifetime.

At times we may think we have seen dramatic instances of persuasion: Churchill in Britain, Hitler in Germany. But we should always ask how much of the behavior we witnessed was the product of persuasive speech. Remember that Churchill was not moving his audience from one end of a belief continuum to the other. The true measure of persuasion is the *change* that is produced. When any speaker addresses partisans, a reaction is likely. Few Democrats can fail to get applause from other Democrats; but assessing the true measure of influence in these cases is difficult.

Of Hitler's Germany we might ask: how much of the observed reaction was due to the influence of his persuasive speaking; how much of the reaction was due to threats and resulting fears, the witnessing of physical violence, and the suppression of any opposing viewpoints; and, to what degree was Hitler a persuadee, or at least to what extent did he simply develop existing conditions. It is difficult to determine the roles played by the influence of his speech, the influences of coercive factors in the situation, and the values and aspirations of German society at the time.

One should not, however, jump to the conclusion that there is no such thing as influential discourse. It would be difficult to argue that Churchill and Hitler had no persuasive effect. It is necessary, though, to put this matter in proper perspective. As one reviews the history of the United States, he sees persuasive speaking and persuasive influence at every turn. He sees it in movements such as the American Revolution, the agrarian revolt, and the civil rights agitation. He sees it in men such as Alexander Hamilton, Daniel Webster, Wendell Phillips, Franklin D. Roosevelt, and Martin Luther King, Jr. As these examples may indicate, the influence of persuasive speak-

4. Bernard Berelson and Gary A. Steiner, *Human Behavior: An Inventory of Scientific Findings* (New York: Harcourt, Brace & World, Inc., 1964), pp. 287, 542, and 575.

ing is greatest when it serves to focus the impact of other social forces. In isolation, the effect of persuasive discourse is limited and transitory; but it may be extremely potent as the cutting edge of forces already tending toward some social action or change. We may contrast two popular images of the persuader: on one hand, the image of the diabolical manipulator shaping and molding people toward his own ends entirely through the clever manipulation of mass persuasion techniques; on the other hand, the image of a "great leader" working through mass persuasion to focus existing social forces toward specific ends consistent with the goals and values of the society. The first image, though it makes good fiction, is false; for unless such a diabolical manipulator is able to control other essential segments of social life, his persuasive machinations will avail him little. The second image, recalling a Churchill and a Hitler, is essentially valid. In short, persuasive influence seems greatest in those circumstances where many conditions in the society have prepared the way and provided the opportunity for a strong leader to exercise the persuasive ability he commands.

Let us now turn to more detail regarding the nature of persuasive influence. In the preceding chapter, we outlined a system of value structures, and we emphasized the general and pervasive nature of these systems. An "economic" man becomes such as a result of years of adapting to and learning in his particular environment. Such a value system is relatively impervious to a persuasive attack and would take about as long to change as it did to develop. But even though making a change in the broad economic value is unlikely, it is possible to effect some change in a specific economic proposition of limited scope.

As we said before, our commitment to a proposition is the product of our beliefs, or considerations of *probableness* of events, and our attitudes, or considerations of *affect* toward events. A realistic aim for persuasive speaking is that it will modify a listener's beliefs and/or affects toward the proposition advanced by the speaker. To influence an "economic" man who opposes any relations with Red China, we might present a message that would increase the degree to which he considers trade with Red China as *probably* beneficial to the economy of the United States. To the extent that we could modify his views of *probable* benefit of such action to the United States, we might influence his behavior. We could achieve a similar end by presenting material which would modify his *affect* or feeling toward Red China, for any message that would increase the degree to which he feels favorable to Red China could influence his behavior. Such influences on specific beliefs and attitudes are quite possible as a result of persuasive speaking.

As stated in the last chapter, these modifications of position can be considered as resulting from learning that is reinforced; that is, the new views are accompanied by factors which reward their acceptance. The release of tensions that comes with accepting the new position, the comfort of the cognitive balance so achieved, the pleasantness of association with the prestigious advocate, or the hope of future personal gain, may all serve as rewards which, for the moment at least, will tend to "fix" or "set" the modified viewpoint.

One further question must be raised regarding the nature of persuasive speaking influence: How is the end of this process accomplished; what is the essence of the persuasive process? The best available evidence suggests that the influence or effect resulting from persuasive speaking should be viewed as a change in the object of judgment. In the situation above, for example, it is not so much a *new judgment* of Red China that results as it is a new *Red China* which is being judged. The concept or category or set of feelings and beliefs associated with Red China is changed; in other words, the "meaning" of Red China for the persuadee is modified. This conception of the influence of persuasive speaking is a central point in the view of persuasion being presented here. It is consistent with our discussion in the previous chapter concerning the dynamic and tentative nature of our categorizing and labeling processes, and it has many implications for our discussion of the consequences of persuasive speaking in the final chapter of this book. Consider the statement:

> I hold it that a little rebellion, now and then, is a good thing, and as necessary in the political world as storms are in the physical.

When told that this statement was by Thomas Jefferson, subjects tended to agree with it and interpreted the word *rebellion* as "minor agitation." When the statement was attributed to Lenin, subjects tended to disagree with it and interpreted *rebellion* as meaning "revolution." S. E. Asch[5] asserts that the differing responses should not be explained in terms of the *same* statement being evaluated differently because of the suggestive power of the author's names. Rather, two *dissimilar* statements are being evaluated. It is not the judgments of the object (statement) that are dissimilar, but rather the objects of judgment. This conception is crucial in our approach to persuasion and will be developed further in the following chapter.

Our view of persuasive speaking influence, then, is that the potential for such influence is somewhat limited. To the extent that it

5. An interested reader may wish to follow up this point by referring to the article by Solomon E. Asch listed in the Recommended Readings.

occurs, persuasion results from changed beliefs and attitudes toward propositions. These changes produce modifications in the concepts and associations which make up the proposition. They represent modifications in "meaning," the final result of which is a change in the object of judgment. Changes in the belief and attitude compo-nents of category systems and the resulting modification of those systems, then, are the ends or goals of persuasive speaking.

4.

THE PERSUASIVE

SPEAKING PROCESS

We have discussed the antecedents to persuasion and a view of the occasion and of the end of persuasive discourse. We can now turn to a detailed analysis of the dynamics by which, within the framework of the occasion, the antecedents lead to the ends. There are four major phases or processes which bind together the persuader, the persuadee, and the persuasive message. These four phases are Receiving, Focusing, Associating, and Resolving. The gerundial form is used to emphasize the ongoing nature of these processes—they should be viewed as processes and not as static products. For instance, the label "Receiving" will carry the feeling of activity, whereas "Reception" might better be interpreted as the end result of the activity. Although the four phases will appear in some ways to be chronological stages, they are not strictly so. They may occur simultaneously for the duration of the persuasive speech. It is important to always keep in mind the constant interaction among these phases and between the participants throughout the persuasive process.

RECEIVING

The phase of Receiving has to do with the process by which a spoken persuasive message is perceived by a listener. We have already pointed out that persuasive messages can only be transmitted, never transferred. Because the receiver of a persuasive speech is human, and not a tape recorder, there are *two* persuasive messages in every persuasion setting — the message sent and the message received. A listener contributes much to the persuasive message he receives. He and the speaker in many ways may be said to be co-creators in the situation. More will be said about this in the next chapter when we discuss the responsibilities and ethics involved in speaking. At this point, however, we need to discuss the process by which a persuasive message is received.

There are two major ways in which a message is modified as it is received: it is *filtered,* and it is *completed* by the listener. Filtering may occur in a number of ways. At the most obvious level, if a listener is slightly hard of hearing, he may miss some of the speech, perhaps a great portion of it. Suppose that a listener is foreign born and is only now acquiring the use of English as a second language. The vocabulary or syntax in some parts of the speech might be confusing for him, and he may not receive them. Another listener might be intellectually dull, another sleepy, and still another more concerned with a problem he must face tomorrow. For any of these reasons, large portions of the transmitted message may simply not be received.

Other types of filtering are more subtle. Suppose we were to perform an experiment in which we presented to a general audience a speech that advances some arguments favoring the Democratic party and some arguments favoring the Republican party. We then administer a retention test to all members of the audience. What would you expect to happen? In essence, this experiment has been carried out a number of times, and the findings generally coincide. The Democrats in the audience will tend to remember more of the material favoring their position, and the Republicans will tend to remember more of the material favoring their views. This result will occur even when the audience is cautioned prior to the speech to remember all of the content for a test to be given immediately following the speech.

In an early study of this type, a ten-minute speech was presented which contained equal amounts of material favorable and unfavorable to the New Deal. Three groups of subjects listened to the speech: a group favorable to the New Deal, a group with neutral feelings toward the New Deal, and a group unfavorable to the New Deal. Following the speech, a recognition test was given which contained equal numbers of items (23 each) from the favorable and unfavorable material. The table below shows the mean number of pro-New Deal and anti-New Deal items recognized by each of the three groups. From the table, the effects of filtering during the receiving process are evident. Subjects favorable to the New Deal remembered more pro material, and subjects with the opposite bias remembered better the anti-New Deal statements:

	PRO-NEW DEAL ITEMS RECOGNIZED	ANTI-NEW DEAL ITEMS RECOGNIZED
Subjects favorable to New Deal	16.1	9.9
Subjects neutral to New Deal	12.8	11.8
Subjects unfavorable to New Deal	10.9	13.0

The study concludes:

> . . . it is almost impossible to expect objectivity and accuracy in perception, learning, remembering, thinking, etc., when ego-involved frames of reference are stimulated. Our behavior is too much determined by our desires, wishes, beliefs, attitudes, and values for us to expect anything other than what we find, namely, highly subjective responses.[1]

Studies on selective perception phenomena such as this indicate that a transmitted message will be filtered by a listener's needs, by his expectations, and by his prior knowledge. If a man is hungry, he may focus on that part of a message which promises food and fail to hear the part outlining the violence needed to get it. And it is not surprising that a partisan will receive better and retain longer those items in a speech with which he is familiar.

A second major way in which a message is modified during the process of Receiving is the completing of messages. Studies of human perception indicate that we tend to see events as wholes, as complete. If we see the figure below, for example, we tend to complete it and see it as a circle. If adjacent dots of light flicker alter-

1. Allen L. Edwards, "Rationalization in Recognition as a Result of a Political Frame of Reference," *Journal of Abnormal and Social Psychology*, XXXVI (April 1941), 224–235.

nately, we may see movement. In this "phi phenomenon" we complete our perceptual experience by adding intermediate dots of light and the sensation of motion. It is not a process of filtering something out of a message that we are witnessing in these cases but rather a process of adding something to a message as it is received.

Studies of learning by conditioning have shown an effect which has been termed *stimulus generalization*. Once a conditioned response has been established for a given stimulus, that response may be elicited not only by the controlled stimulus but also by a variety of similar stimuli. If a person is conditioned to react in a certain manner following the presentation of a 1000-cycle tone, he will later respond similarly to tones close to 1000 cycles per second.

Completing behavior of this type can be observed in a persuasive speaking setting. In a study conducted by this writer,[2] for example, subjects listened to a speech arguing against the expansion of federal government power into the areas of health and education. The persons persuaded by the speech were also found to have transferred some of the effect of the speech; they were also influenced against the expansion of federal power in other specific areas, such as agriculture and water power resources. This generalizing or transferring effect is one aspect of a person's tendency to seek internal consistency and completeness. If a person is persuaded on two or three specific cases, he tends to complete the category (generalize) by adding other related cases. Man does this because of the need to provide order to his existence, as described in Chapter 2. Such categorizing behavior is considered here as a process of completing a persuasive message as it is received.

Once again, individual needs, expectations, and previous experiences will influence the process of completing what is seen and heard. In a speaking situation, if we expect "illogical ranting" from that "buffoon on the platform," we will probably hear it. If we approve of his viewpoint, we may see the distant speaker as taller or handsomer than he might otherwise appear. If he says something which might be objectionable coming from another, we might paraphrase, "When he said . . . , he meant . . . ." In this interpretative manner we often add to a transmitted message.

In a study conducted by Hovland and Sherif, Negro and white students were asked to scale various statements about Negroes by placing them along a continuum of "favorableness to Negroes."[3] The

---

2. Thomas M. Scheidel, "An Exploratory Study of the Relationships Between Certain Organismic Variables and Response to a Persuasive Speech" (Seattle, 1958). An unpublished Doctoral dissertation.
3. Sherif and Hovland, op. cit., pp. 99–126.

statements were intended to range widely in expressed sentiment from "pro-Negro" through "neutral" to "anti-Negro." The hypotheses, which were generally confirmed, were that Negro students would concentrate their placements of the statements into a smaller number of prescribed categories than would students for whom the issue was less ego-involving, and that this bunching of items would tend to occur in the extreme categories. In short, it was found that the Negro subjects displaced the neutral items toward the anti-Negro end of the continuum.

The explanation offered was that individuals who are highly ego-involved in an issue are most discriminating in placing items in a category representing their own stand, but they bunch together all statements differing from their own stand at the end of the scale they reject. Why would this happen? The best answer seems to be that an ego-involved person completes the meaning of "neutral" statements by adding negative elements to them. In his past experience, those who have made "neutral" comments toward him have been indifferent to him or perhaps have opposed him but have been "tactful" in his presence. In many ways, persons who are neutral toward us pose more of a threat to our self-esteem than do persons who oppose us. The negative impressions gained from these past experiences are added to the "neutral" statements.

Filtering and completing are essential features of listening behavior; without them verbal communication would be extremely cumbersome. Even though they may lead to distortion and error, they contribute much to the efficiency of communication and so become a part of everyone's listening habits. In particular, completing is necessary because all language is abstract and abbreviated. The whole of the matter can never be transmitted during the course of any speech, and the speaker must always rely upon his listener to supply some missing data. Every listener will filter and add to what is transmitted. These processes dramatize the role played by the persuadee in persuasion. They show how he enters dynamically into the process in the very first stages. The aspect of Receiving is especially significant in explaining persuasive effects on partisans, or those persons strongly committed to a position. The process of filtering explains their lack of response to opposing viewpoints; they do not receive them. Conversely, their response to fellow partisans is explained in part by completing. If favorable to a position, the persuadee needs only the slightest stimulation in that direction. He will add to the message and, in fact, contribute greatly to his own persuasion. This thought helps explain our example of Churchill, as a war leader, addressing a highly sympathetic audience. As Churchill himself commented,

It was the nation and the race dwelling around the globe that
had the lion's heart. I had the luck to be called upon to give
the roar.

FOCUSING

A need for some degree of order seems basic to human behavior. The
aspect of Focusing has to do with the manner in which a persuasive
message is organized and emphasized. Depending upon the proposition and the purpose of a speech, certain ideas will be superordinate,
many will be coordinate, and still others subordinate. The ideas
should be complete and cover the proposition, and they should cohere
and be mutually consistent. These requirements of organization may
be planned and imposed by the speaker. If not, or if the planning was
not appropriate for the audience, then the listener may provide his
own order to the message. Once again, his needs, expectations, and
experiences will influence the ordering. A major purpose of organization is to provide clarity by means of focus or emphasis.

As a message is received, it is narrowed, and parts of it stand out
more clearly than other parts. These emphasized portions receive the
greatest attention from the listener. It is common for writers on
persuasion to discuss attention. Cornell's James Winans did; so did
Hovland, Janis, and Kelley in the synthesis of their early studies at
Yale. In many works on persuasion, attention is discussed as a necessary precondition if persuasion is to occur. But the mechanism
explaining why or how attention leads to persuasive influence is not
often made very clear. We will consider what focusing is and how it
is produced by the interaction of persuader and persuadee. We will go
further to present a view of the role of Focusing in persuasive speaking; specifically, that in the persuasive speaking situation, Focusing
will necessarily create persuasive effect.

Consider a speaking situation. The persuader who is opposed to a
certain proposal may spend the greatest share of his attack upon it
discussing financial considerations, the amount of money required
and the difficulties of obtaining it. He focuses on the economics of
the issue. But suppose that the listener is most concerned with the
question of social justice and that he was discussing and thinking of
this aspect of the issue just prior to hearing the speech. In this situation, even though the speaker may spend only a few minutes on the
question of social justice, the listener supplies the focus, and social
justice is the emphasis of the speech for him.

How can speaker and listener supply differing focus to a speech?
What is focus, and what gives emphasis to a speech? Studies in

human psychology have found that sensation is a matter of energy change. A perfectly homogeneous and unchanging environment is equivalent to no sensation at all. Difference and change provide emphasis or focus. Mount Rainier, near Seattle, commands one's attention (on a clear day) because it differs so from its immediate surroundings. It literally stands apart from its environment. Many of the individual peaks in the Canadian Rockies are higher than Rainier, but they are not nearly so impressive because they do not differ from their surroundings. One peak among many is not emphasized; a single peak, standing by itself, draws our attention.

How can a speaker provide focus in his speech? Some speakers shout their speeches, intending to add emphasis. But when all the speech is shouted, there is no emphasis. So we cannot say that increased volume necessarily will give emphasis. Neither can we say that a dramatic gesture necessarily will provide emphasis. We can say that an action which differs markedly from a speaker's norm will accomplish this end, however. Any *change* in pace or pattern will help a speaker achieve a measure of emphasis.

A speaker has many ways for providing focus in these terms. The primary characteristic of emphasis is the conflict in cognitions or the incongruity between what the listener has expected and what he receives. The incongruity between the words and the inflection in Mark Antony's "For Brutus is an honorable man" gives focus and meaning. Repetition of ideas and asides to an audience, such as "Now this is an important point," will emphasize those thoughts. The speaker may also use rhetorical questions, metaphor, and humor as emphatic devices.

The rhetorical question provides focus, because a question always calls for implicit audience response. William Wirt's account of Patrick Henry's speech to the Virginia House of Burgesses contains this series of questions:

But when shall we be stronger?
Shall we gather strength by irresolution and inaction?
Why stand we here idle?
What is it that gentlemen wish?
Is life so dear, or peace so sweet, as to be purchased at the price
of chains and slavery?[4]

Can you imagine an audience unmoved by such questioning?

Use of metaphor can add visualization and concreteness to an otherwise abstract thought. The juxtaposing of concrete and abstract

4. *The World's Great Speeches*, ed. Lewis Copeland (Garden City, N. Y.: Garden City Publishing Company, Inc., 1942), pp. 233–234.

can be impressive. At the grave of his brother, Robert G. Ingersoll visualizes and softens a premature death by this means.

> Yet, after all, it may be best, just in the happiest, sunniest hour of all the voyage, while eager winds are kissing every sail, to dash against the unseen rock, and in an instant hear the billows roar above a sunken ship. For, whether in midsea or 'mong the breakers of the farther shore, a wreck at last must mark the end of each and all. And every life, no matter if its every hour is rich with love and every moment jeweled with a joy, will, at its close, become a tragedy as sad and deep and dark as can be woven of the warp and woof of mystery and death.[5]

Humor can also be an effective way of providing focus. Unfortunately, in too many speeches humor is included only in the form of jokes in the introduction. The speaker may gain audience attention in the introduction which lasts only during the introduction. This is almost certain to happen to the speaker who moves from a humorous introduction with the transition, ". . . and now turning to my speech." But when appropriate to the occasion and when well used throughout a speech, humor can be very effective. Like all the other types of focus employed by a speaker, humor is based upon the unexpected, upon a conflict between the expected and the observed.

In addition to the focus provided by the speaker, the listener will inevitably provide a focus of his own. He will hear best those statements which are relevant to his needs, his expectations, and his experiences. They will be emphasized by him. The skillful speaker, aware of this fact, will take these sources of emphasis into account in adapting his message to his audience. As a listener provides emphasis, he contributes to his own persuasion and helps the speaker achieve his ends. The manner in which a persuadee filters and completes any persuasive message has been pointed out. The same motives, values, and reasoning processes account for the focusing phenomenon.

Although this type of listener behavior is often indispensable to the speaker's purpose, it can be troublesome if a funny story or an interesting fact receives greater response from a listener and is better remembered than the main point of the speech. One of the most difficult tasks of a speaker is to focus his audience's attention upon his major ideas and to prevent them from giving too much attention to less vital introductory and amplifying materials which

5. Ibid., p. 324.

happen to capture their fancy. The surface aspects of any message are often perceived first, and it is not easy for a speaker to focus audience attention on the deeper meaning of his message. It is not surprising that when a person is commenting upon a speech event, he will often discuss physical appearance, voice, and the most apparent aspects of speech style before discussing the ideas of the speech—if indeed he gets to this last point at all.

The process of Focusing is especially helpful in explaining certain aspects of persuasive effect. The typical experimental study of persuasive speaking finds a moderate but significant shift in audience attitude in the direction advocated by the persuader. The shift occurs immediately following the speech. Then as time passes, the attitude of the persuadee tends to shift back toward his original position, even when he gives no further conscious thought to the persuasive appeal. How can we account for such a shift? Certainly, any theory of persuasion should be able to explain such a common finding of research studies.

We have already maintained that the goal of persuasion is the changing of a category system. Emphasis given to parts of a persuasive message will refocus the elements of a category and, while the refocusing lasts, can change the meaning of the category for the persuadee. Perhaps an example will make the point clearer. Anyone may have a number of beliefs and attitudes concerning Russia. Because of previous learning, his many beliefs will be held with varying degrees of attributed probableness. His many attitudes toward Russia will be held with varying degrees of affect. Then, too, his several beliefs and attitudes will each be held with differing degrees of salience or prominence. At any given moment, his "meaning" of the category "Russia" will be the product of all these beliefs and attitudes weighted by their degrees of prominence.

Suppose this person listens to a persuasive speech which emphasizes beliefs and attitudes favorable to Russia. Such a speech may refocus the attentions of the persuadee to those favorable beliefs and attitudes and momentarily de-emphasize his negative reactions. As the favorable views gain increased salience, the overall meaning of the category "Russia" will, for the time, be more favorable, and a persuasive effect will be apparent. But when the speech ends, the particular emphases it added will immediately begin to fade. When the distracting influence of the speech ends and our persuadee returns to his regular and usual environment, the relative salience of each of his beliefs and attitudes will tend to return to what it was before hearing the speech. Having been learned over a long period of time, those original views tend to be relatively stable. The observed persuasive effect may then appear to fade.

As this example shows, Focusing is at least temporary persuasion. Emphasis gives new focus to certain elements within a category. As long as the focus exists, the category may be restructured, and persuasion will be effected. But after the speaking situation and the emphasis it provides have ended, the original and prevailing category structure will tend to return, and the persuasive influence will begin to fade. In this manner then, Focusing is most helpful in explaining the persuasion process. Whereas receiving accounts especially for the persuasion of partisans, Focusing provides a more general explanation. Focusing can explain adequately the influence on those persuadees with less favorable initial attitudes. While this is an important distinction, the parallels between Receiving and Focusing should be recognized. In both processes we see the interaction of persuader and persuadee. Both contribute to the final product. Both determine, in part, what is received and what is emphasized in a persuasive message.

ASSOCIATING

Associating is an aspect of the persuasion process which stands a bit apart from Receiving and Focusing and serves as a bridge between them and Resolving. Associating is the process by which a category system is restructured. Since we are defining persuasive effect as a change in the object of judgment, category restructuring is the essence of persuasion. Our explanation in this section will be that the restructuring of concepts and categories is largely a product of newly established or re-formed associations. We will attempt to show here how these associations are manipulated to effect persuasion.

Two different dimensions of Associating are important in the persuasive speaking process. The first is the relating of specific beliefs and attitudes in different and new patterns. This aspect focuses upon the message elements transmitted and received. The second is the relating of persuader and persuadee to one another. This aspect focuses upon the personalities conjoined in the persuasive speaking situation.

In Chapter 1 we mentioned psychological consistency theories. There are a number of such theories:[6] Heider's "tendency toward balance," Newcomb's "stress toward symmetry," Festinger's "cognitive dissonance," and Osgood and Tannenbaum's "tendency toward increased congruity," among others. While distinctions may be drawn among these viewpoints, they share many common elements. Perhaps some additional explanation will be helpful. Generally the

6. The interested reader may find a summary and comparison of these theories in Roger Brown's book in the Recommended Readings.

consistency theory posits that man has a tendency to seek internal consistency in his cognitions, harmony in his associations. The theory further holds that imbalance or dissonance is a motivating force, driving one to seek a new balance. Suppose that a highly respected speaker advocates a cause we do not favor. Our feelings toward the speaker and our feelings toward the cause are in conflict. According to consistency theory, the existence of this conflict will motivate us to modify our cognitions in one of a number of ways. We may become more favorable toward the cause, or we may lower our esteem of the speaker, or we may say that we did not hear the speaker correctly or that he did not intend what we heard, or, in the extreme, we may repress the entire experience. Consistency theory thus provides a motivating force for harmony, although it does not explain just how that force leads to a change in position.

Let us consider some ways in which association of beliefs and attitudes leads to a restructuring of concepts or categories. Persuasion may occur when the persuader associates a concept he is advancing with a concept already favored by the persuadee. We have all heard speakers do this. The speaker may relate two ideas, "The Bible commands us to love all men; the civil rights movement asks us to show love for all men." In this way the speaker associates the category of his cause (civil rights movement) with another category (the Bible). The two become associated with one another because both are shown to be associated with a common third category (love of all men).

To be sure, if judged by the standards of formal logic, the "premises" do not lead to the "conclusion"; in fact, judged as a sample of logical reasoning, this chain of association is an example of a well-known logical fallacy, "the fallacy of the Undistributed Middle." But it would be a mistake to judge this associative chain as an example of logical reasoning or to assume that its psychological impact is in any way related to its logical adequacy. In all probability, if the category (Bible) is evaluated highly by the listener, and if the association is received, then the action of "loving all men" should become a salient or dominant aspect of the category (civil rights movement), and the positive affect or feeling toward "love all men" should transfer from (the Bible) to (the civil rights movement). This association may represent either an addition to or a changed emphasis within the category. The added evaluative factor, coupled with its salience in the category (civil rights movement), would modify the meaning of that category for the listener, and the new meaning of the category would include more aspects of favorableness. In this manner, Associating modifies the meaning of the category. Changing the object of judgment, it results in persuasive influence.

Let us analyze another example of Associating which appears frequently—the use of expert testimony. We have all watched television commercials for a certain razor blade showing the sincere testimony given by a popular baseball player. This situation is so contrived that even children pick up the weakness in the argument. However strained, the attempt here clearly is persuasion by association. And this technique can be used with effect.

Suppose a respected authority figure speaks out in favor of a proposed new program for aid to Latin America. The category (respected authority X) is brought into association with the category (program Y). Suppose you have a number of beliefs and attitudes about X. You believe he is honest, expert, reliable, trustworthy, unbiased. Your feelings toward him as a person are highly favorable. You know little about program Y. Since the "meaning" of program Y for you is the category made up of all the beliefs and attitudes you hold concerning it, your category (program Y) is vague and incomplete. But the persuasive speaking situation has strongly associated your category X with your category Y. Category Y will tend to take on some of the meaning of X by this association. You will likely tend to consider program Y to be a fair and just program and to hold a fairly high evaluation of it. Again the object of judgment (program Y) has been changed by adding new elements to that category and by emphasizing favorable elements. This transfer has been made possible by the association of concepts X and Y and by our natural tendency to seek harmony, congruity, and symmetry in our associations. The need for balance provides the impetus, and the association of somewhat disparate categories provides the situation for persuasion. Some elements of the categories are fused or transferred, and the meanings of those categories are thereby modified. In that modification, we have the fact of persuasion.

We could go on drawing example after example of this occurrence where the concept that is the subject of the persuasive speech is associated with another concept evaluated favorably by the persuadee, but perhaps these two examples have made the point. It should be easy to see how two concepts can be associated, how a concept can be associated with a certain authority figure, how an unknown speaker may be related to a listener's general concept of authority figures, and so on. The rationale for the persuasion effected in every case would be the same.

There is yet another manner of associating beliefs and affects into new patterns. Although the explanation for the resulting persuasion will not differ from the cases above, this pattern should be mentioned. In the cases above, one category was purposefully associated with another category considered to be highly favorable in the view of the listener. It should be clear that one could also create associations with categories considered unfavorably by the listener.

An effective means of persuasion is the technique of bringing to the surface for the persuadee two concepts he holds equally favorably and showing how they conflict. Suppose the cause is integration and the persuadee is a segregationist who also is a businessman with high economic values. A speech might be persuasive if it demonstrated that segregation depresses an economy. In this way, some conflicts would be drawn between the category (segregation) and the category (good business). From our discussion above, it should be clear how these categories could be restructured in line with the purpose of the persuader.

A special application of this technique is found in the dialectic method of argument. Socrates was supposed to have used this method in his teaching, and, if accurately exemplified in Plato's dialogues, he certainly used it in his persuading. This question and answer technique does just what we have been describing. It tends to guide the pupil or antagonist in bringing his categories to the surface and allowing him to see conflict in his associations.

Thus far we have discussed associations of belief and attitude elements in categories considered in persuasive messages. Another dimension in the Associating process has to do with the personalities involved in the persuasive speaking situation. The relating of persuader and persuadee with one another is of great importance in the total process. The association of individuals, just as the association of ideas, can lead to persuasive influence.

Kenneth Burke, who has written extensively on persuasion, centers his theory on the key term *identification.*

> A is not identical with his colleague B. But insofar as their interests are joined, A is *identified* with B. . . . Yet at the same time he remains unique, an individual locus of motives. Thus he is both joined and separate, at once a distinct substance and consubstantial with another.[7]

We say sometimes that persons have good rapport with one another, that one man has empathy with another. All of this may sound somewhat mystical, but perhaps it need not. An analogy from the physical world may help. We know of sympathetic vibration. If one of two tuning forks of equal frequency placed near each other is struck and then its vibration is stopped, a sound will be heard from the second fork. It has been set into sympathetic vibration by the very

7. Kenneth Burke, *A Grammar of Motives and a Rhetoric of Motives,* Meridan edition (Cleveland: The World Publishing Company, 1962), pp. 544–545.

small amount of energy in the sound waves from the first fork. If the second tuning fork is of a different frequency from the first, this phenomenon will not occur. Sympathetic vibration can also be produced with piano strings of the same frequency. And we know that delicate glassware can be shattered if a sufficiently intense sound happens to be identical with the resonant frequency of the glass; as it is set into strong sympathetic vibration, the glass shatters. The necessary condition for sympathetic vibration is that the two bodies have identical resonant frequencies.

This physical principle is analogous to two individuals with similar psychological "resonant frequencies." If they are brought into association, there seems to be a natural tendency for one to respond to the other. They have many factors in common, and they seem to respond to many events similarly. One of the general findings of behavioral science research in persuasion is that a person is most persuaded and influenced by his close friends and associates and by his family. Voting behavior, for example, seems to be determined to a greater extent by parental predispositions than by the persuasive speaking in any single election campaign. Of course, the fact of constant contact for a long period of time with parents and friends is one reason for this result. But another reason is the factor of association.

Persons who have good rapport sometimes speak in a jargon which greatly abbreviates their messages. They can each count on the other's ability to fill in a cryptic message with appropriate details. In Tolstoy's novel *Anna Karenina*, the two lovers communicate by using the initial letters of each word, such as I−l−y−. Two persons with many common experiences will tend to develop similar categories and strategies for reasoning, and, studies have found, persons with similar backgrounds will likely have similar connotations for language symbols. These facts make the effects of association possible. In the process of persuasion, Associating could well be the most influential aspect.

To explain the effect of this interpersonal association, we can draw upon two concepts from classical rhetorical theory. The first concept is that of the *topoi*, or "topics," or "places of arguments." Widely used in ancient times, the lists of topics were lists of standard and possible arguments that a persuader should consider as he selects the arguments he will use in any given persuasive situation. The topics were *special*, relating to specific concerns, or *general*, applicable in all sorts of persuasive cases. If a man is speaking on legal matters, the special topics of right and wrong and of justice and equity are among those which he should consider for use. The special topics were simply those usual matters of concern relevant to the issue under discussion. The general topics were possible approaches to any topic. Aristotle lists such possibilities as more and less, magnifying and minifying, past and future, possible and impossible. Cicero considers consistency and inconsistency, similarity and dissimilarity, cause and effect, among others. According to his purpose, the speaker might choose to magnify the problem or to minimize it. He might concentrate on its causes or upon its effects. By considering each of these topics in turn, as they relate to the issue he plans to advocate, the persuasive speaker would be aided in selecting appropriate materials. He could guard against overlooking an effective argument by means of such a survey.

In our terms, *topoi* are the categories and strategies employed by a persuader. We will not attempt here a listing of all possible lines of argument, though a modern system of *topoi* might be helpful. What we want to suggest is that if a persuader and a persuadee are brought into association, persuasive influence will depend to a large degree upon the extent to which speaker and listener employ similar topics; i.e., common categories and strategies. To some degree, this commonness is under the direct control of the persuader. He may adapt and attempt to "speak the language" of his listener. Addressing a Methodist women's club, he may speak in terms of religion and the home. He may relate his proposition to categories of religious experience and family life. If later in the day he speaks to the local Junior Chamber of Commerce, he may relate the same proposition to categories of economic concern. The speaker would be less effective if he attempted to give the same speech in the two settings. And merely adjusting the introductory material of the speech is not enough. This type of adaptation enables a speaker to approach more closely the sympathetic association between persuader and persuadee which facilitates persuasive influence. We must say, however, that to a large degree this mutual sympathetic responsiveness is a product of the basic nature of the individuals and is not amenable to change in a single persuasive speaking situation.

A second term from classical rhetoric, helpful in explaining interpersonal influence, is *stasis*, or the "status of the case." Cicero and Quintilian taught that the status of a case can be determined by asking questions: whether a thing is, what it is, and of what kind it is. Does the case focus on a question of fact, or of definition, or of quality? For example, let us take a hypothetical case in which A is accused of murdering B. The first question (fact) asks, did A kill B? The second question (definition) asks, did the killing of B fit our legal definition of murder? The third question (quality) asks, was the act good or bad; was it justified? We can see that, at any given moment, the focus of the argument might fall on one or the other of these states. The issue might be, did A kill B? If that is proven, then the issue could become, was it an act of murder? In Cicero's defense of Milo the fact that Milo killed Clodius was admitted. It was not the point at issue. But the case turned on definition. Since Clodius attacked Milo, the killing was one of self-defense and not murder.

The importance of *stasis* for the interpersonal association of persuader and persuadee lies in the fact that if persuader and persuadee are to be in close association, they must see the status of a given case similarly. No persuasion will occur if the speaker is belaboring an issue already accepted by the listener. If the listener is to respond maximally, the speaker must sense and concentrate upon the particular concerns, needs, and expectations of the listener at that moment; otherwise the listener will not respond by associating. The degree to which the speaker is capable of this adaptation will determine the degree of his influence. We see once more the interaction of speaker and listener in the persuasive process; both contribute to this association. The speaker may instigate the process and make attempts at adaptation, but the nature of the listener and the influence of that nature cannot be excluded from the process.

One other aspect of Associating which plays a role in persuasion is the association of persuadee with fellow members of groups to which he belongs. We have discussed earlier how one's judgments may be influenced by mob action occurring around him. In this event, the association of one with others in an audience may, in itself, have persuasive effect. Even if private and individual judgments are made, group membership may have persuasive effect. In one study, for example, a questionnaire containing some items opposing norms of the Roman Catholic faith was administered to two groups of Catholic students. One group was informed that they all were Catholics, the other group was not. What would you expect to happen? The results showed that subjects in the first group answered the critical items in the questionnaire more in line with the positions prescribed for Catholics than did the second group.[8] The salience or prominence of group membership influenced the persuadees to follow the norms of that group more closely.

Throughout our treatment of persuasive speaking, we have attempted to weave the classical modes of proof (character, reason, emotion) into patterns more meaningful for our day. In Chapter 2, reasoning was defined as the association of labels one has applied to categories of his experience. Inference was described as the associa-

8. For more information about this and similar studies see chapter on "Group Membership and Resistance to Influence" in Carl I. Hovland, Irving L. Janis, and Harold H. Kelley, *Communication and Persuasion* (New Haven: Yale University Press, 1953).

tion of particulars through the processes of categorizing and generalizing. It is the view here that *reasoning* in the persuasive speaking setting occurs as the Associating process.

Associating is a key element in the persuasive process. As ideas of the persuader are associated with ideas of the persuadee, categories are restructured and persuasion occurs. When the persuader and persuadee associate as persons, when they respond similarly to the concepts and strategies of the persuasive message, and when they simultaneously focus on the various states of the case, persuasion occurs.

RESOLVING

The final phase in the persuasive speaking process is Resolving. This aspect bears primarily upon the fixing of the persuasive influence. So far we have discussed the manner in which Receiving, Focusing, and Associating result in restructured categories of experience, redefined meanings for concepts, and changed objects of judgment. How are these modifications fixed or set? We have already noted the tendency for a listener to move toward his original position as time passes following a persuasive speech. Some effects do remain, however, and in this section we shall present some explanation for this lingering influence.

We must remember that Receiving, Focusing, and Associating occur only *during* the persuasive speaking event. Once the speaking situation comes to an end, the reception ends, and the emphasis and associations fade; persuasive influence fades. But we all know that some persuasive effects are lasting. How can the continuing influence of a persuasive speech be explained in terms that are consistent with our previous comments about transitory influences? Learning theory seems to provide the basis for a reasonable explanation. Lasting effects are likely due to the *learning* of some aspects of the restructured belief and attitude systems. As we noted in our discussion of learning by reinforcement, behavior patterns which are rewarded generally tend to be repeated.

Consider the case of a person who hears a speech presenting views favorable toward Russia and is persuaded to a more favorable position. At the moment of the speech event, his category "Russia" might be restructured because of (1) the presentation of previously unknown facts from a reliable source, (2) an emphasis by the speaker upon values held strongly by the listener, (3) the association occurring as the listener identifies with the Russian people, and (4) the effects of the prestige of the speaker. All these causes for restructuring the meaning of "Russia" combine to produce a marked persuasive effect. As time passes, so might the influence of items (2) and (4). The emphasis is gone, and the speaker and message may become dissociated. Perhaps item (1) was learned because the listener values knowledge and this value reinforced his retention of the information. Perhaps he has a strong social value and a need for belonging which reinforced his newly experienced association in item (3). In either case, the new patterns of thinking persisted because they were rewarded; that is, because they filled some already existing need or desire.

Adequate rewards for implementing persuasive effect in the Resolving process can be anything meeting the motives and needs of men as outlined in Chapter 2. Consider Maslow's theory of motivation. Any appeal, direct or indirect, immediate or anticipated, which meets a basic and salient need would serve as a reinforcer. Or one might think in terms of Spranger's theory of values: considerations of sympathy for others should be rewarding for the "social" type of man, whereas persons with greater "theoretical" values should consider new information more rewarding, and a potential for personal power should be especially rewarding for one moved primarily by the "political" value.

Through reinforcement, parts of a persuasive experience may be learned. But, as with any learning, the new experiences will undergo extinction, or tend to fade, as time passes unless such experience is repeated and occasionally receives additional reinforcement. The rewards which fix, by learning, some aspects of the persuasive message as it is presented and the process by which this occurs are what we mean to cover with the term Resolving.

The role of the learning process in Resolving is important in yet another way. Whereas a restructured concept may lead to behavior change through learning, the reverse is also true. Behavior change may lead to restructured concepts. Studies have been made of persons who have moved into new groups or taken jobs at higher status levels. In their new roles they tended to behave in a manner demanded by or expected in those roles. In time, these persons developed attitudes that supported their new behavior. For example, one of the findings of enforced integration in the military services was a shift toward more favorable attitudes toward Negroes by men who previously were reluctant to associate with Negroes.

The four phases of the persuasive speaking process presented here are Receiving, Focusing, Associating, and Resolving. Receiving is the process by which a persuasive message is taken in by a listener. It includes the transmission of symbolic cues by a speaker and the modification of the message through filtering and completing by the listener. It serves best to explain persuasive effects upon partisans. Focusing has to do with the manner in which a persuasive speech is organized and emphasized. Focusing produces restructured categories and changes in the object of judgment, which has been defined here as the end of persuasive influence. This phase is helpful as a general explanation of persuasive speaking effects. Associating further describes the ways in which a category system is restructured. Two important aspects of Associating are relating specific beliefs and attitudes in different and new patterns and the relating of the personalities of persuader and persuadee. As with Focusing, Associating provides a general explanation of persuasive influence. Finally, Resolving is the process by which restructured categories are reinforced and thereby learned. Resolving accounts for lasting persuasive effects.

These four phases may occur simultaneously throughout the persuasive speaking process. Each involves the constant interaction and contribution on the part of both persuader and persuadee. Perhaps the chart on the next page which shows how a listener might respond to a sentence from Lincoln's Gettysburg Address will clarify the role of these phases as well as their interactions.

The listener may fail to receive parts of the message, such as "living and dead." It could be that a comment by someone standing near him obscured those words. Or his focus upon the dead, because a cemetery is being dedicated and death is all about him, obscures the thought of "living." The interplay of the phases of persuasion can be seen in this latter instance when Focusing behavior influences Receiving behavior.

Completing may occur if the listener adds elements to the message, such as "from the North and the South." In the present case, one could believe that Lincoln surely was speaking of *all* the brave men who struggled here.

A listener may focus upon parts of the message. If one had some feelings of guilt for not having served in this significant and terrible battle, he might focus upon the juxtaposed ideas of *men who struggled here* and *our poor power*.

In his thinking, a listener may associate this event with others like it in this war or even in all wars, so that Lincoln's thought speaks to a wider audience than that assembled for this specific occasion.

The indirect association with Lincoln allowed by endorsing his views, and the resulting reward and reinforcement, may produce a better retention of the thought. In this manner, Associating can serve the Resolving process.

"The brave men, living and dead, who struggled here, have consecrated it far above our poor power to add or detract."

PHASE	LISTENER'S MESSAGE	POSSIBLE EXPLANATIONS
Receiving-filtering	The brave men, who struggled here, have consecrated it far above our poor power to add or detract.	Listener may not have heard. Listener may have been focusing upon the dead because of his expectations of the occasion.
Receiving-completing	The brave men, from the North and the South, who struggled here, have consecrated it far above our poor power to add or detract.	Listener may add interpretation to message based on his prior knowledge and feelings of Lincoln's position.
Focusing	The brave <u>men</u>, from the North and the South, <u>who struggled here</u>, have consecrated it far above <u>our poor power</u> to add or detract.	Listener may focus on parts of message because of prior beliefs and feelings.
Associating	The brave <u>men</u>, from the North and the South, <u>who struggled here,</u> (as is the case of soldiers who have struggled everywhere), have consecrated it far above <u>our poor power</u> to add or detract.	Listener may generalize by relating this event to other similar occasions.
Resolving	THE BRAVE <u>MEN</u>, FROM THE NORTH AND THE SOUTH, <u>WHO STRUGGLED HERE,</u> (AS IS THE CASE OF SOLDIERS WHO HAVE STRUGGLED EVERYWHERE), HAVE CONSECRATED IT FAR ABOVE <u>OUR POOR POWER</u> TO ADD OR DETRACT.	Listener may find acceptance of message rewarding because of indirect association it allows with an authority figure.

In each phase, the total process is producing a restructured category, a change in meaning for the listener, a change in the object of judgment—or, in other words, persuasive effect. Taken together, these four phases provide an adequate explanation for the various influences observed to result from persuasive discourse.

5.

THE CONSEQUENCES

OF PERSUASIVE SPEAKING

Probably no one of us would maintain that the social act of communication is inherently unethical. Yet we must realize that it is not a neutral force; the very concept of communication implies some degree of influence of one individual over another. The complete autonomy of the listener is denied whenever we succeed in communicating with him. Although he may reject our proposition, there will almost certainly be side-effects because (1) he has been forced to perceive and react to stimuli of our choosing, (2) certain of his categories have been brought into contact with one another, and (3) his attention has been directed to matters of our concern.

From this broad view of the matter, all discourse may be said to be influential. Nor is this a trivial consideration, for it is just this pervasive influence of communication which makes human society possible. Studies of feral and isolated children indicate what man might be, were it not for the communicative act. The few available reports concerning children raised in relative isolation from other humans point to a single striking conclusion: the feral child appears to be "unhuman." His behavior seems more that of an animal than of a human. His "speech" consists largely of grunts and isolated sounds. These findings should not be surprising, for we could hardly expect a person to demonstrate social learning when he has been isolated from society.

The thought of a constant, pervasive influence through all communication may be somewhat disturbing to many of us; yet the thought of an "unhuman" human is likely to be more disturbing.

And it is the influential communicative act which makes "human-ness" possible. The communication process is society's binding and dynamic force. In writing of this influence, George Herbert Mead[1] suggested that each of us develops his concept of *self* as a result of his interaction with others in society, largely in the oral communica-tion setting.

Why is it that these almost self-evident propositions may disturb us? In all probability it is because, as we mentioned earlier, each of us is aware of himself as *subject* but of others as *object*. We often can see the evidences of communicative influence on others; but because our own reactions to communication seem so natural and self-determined, we tend to discount in large measure the influence of other men upon what we are. Communicative influence is not ordinarily detected as such by the listener; and the categories, be-liefs, affects, and other symbolic furniture of the individual are subtly and unconsciously molded to the patterns of the society around him.

These broad implications of communication for the individual and society—what we might call the general social consequences of communication—apply to all forms of communication, whether intentionally influential or not. But they are of special significance to the topic of persuasive speaking, because the persuader, to greater or lesser degree, seeks to accomplish by design what society as a whole does unintentionally. The total consequences of influential discourse and the standards by which we judge those consequences are topics of the greatest importance in our consideration of persuasive speak-ing. This final chapter is devoted to these topics.

POTENTIAL RESULTS OF PERSUASIVE SPEAKING

What are the potential results of persuasive speaking? Consider first the audience. We noted earlier that the outcome of the persuasive speaking encounter generally is evaluated in terms of the extent to which the audience responds to the speaker's proposition as the speaker intended. The persuadee's response to the proposition may range from marked changes of belief and attitude in the direction advocated, through a lack of any apparent change at all, to a nega-tive reaction, or *boomerang effect*.

Although any effect that occurs is more likely to be some degree of positive change, the boomerang effect is not uncommon. In almost

1. George Herbert Mead, *Mind, Self, and Society: From the Standpoint of a Social Behaviorist,* ed. Charles W. Morris (Chicago: University of Chicago Press, 1934). See especially Part III on "Self."

every study of persuasion, a few listeners are found to shift attitudes in directions away from those of the speaker. How can the boomerang effect be explained in terms of the approach to the persuasive speaking process developed in the last chapter? The best explanation traces the effect to a particular focus or association made by the persuadee.

Suppose an encyclopedia salesman comes to your door. He argues that if you take the set and study it carefully, your life will be richer and you may well advance to such a high-salaried position that you can have all the advantages money can buy. But your attention is drawn to the person of this salesman. While you relax at home with your family in the evening, he is traveling door to door in a dark, unfamiliar neighborhood, suffering harassments attendant to his profession, and making an occasional sale to families who he knows can scarcely afford and certainly will not use his product. Why hasn't the man followed his own advice? If the incongruity between the man and what he stands for is your focus at the moment, your response to his argument is neither positive nor neutral, but negative. The boomerang effect occurs not just because of what the persuader says but because of what the persuadee does with the utterance as he receives it within the context of the total situation. In this instance, by adding observations of his own (completing), the persuadee has converted what might otherwise have been a favorable message into an unfavorable one.

Change of listener attitude

Some members of any audience will surely be moved in the direction advocated by the speaker. These positive audience responses to persuasive appeals may be short lived, or they may be more enduring. The explanation for differing results over time follows readily from the discussion in the last chapter. If a persuader is calling for immediate action, as in a speech for charitable contributions or in an appeal for votes in a nominating convention, he usually has only one opportunity for the persuasion, and he is most interested in short-term effects. In such cases the persuader would best consider the processes of Focusing and Associating as they apply to his proposition and he might pay less attention to matters of Resolving. It has been said, for example, that Goldwater's prior association with delegates at the grass-roots level was responsible for his control of votes in the 1964 Republican nominating convention. The effects of Focusing and Associating, without Resolving, are transitory but potent if the desired response follows the persuasive speaking occa-

sion closely in time. If a speaker seeks long-term effects and is able
to engage in a lengthy campaign, he ought to consider the process of
Resolving. He would do well to point up not only the immediate and
direct, but also the potential and indirect rewards associated with the
response he advocates. In this way his audience is more likely to
learn the conditions necessary for the desired response.

The response of the audience to a specific proposition in a speech
is our main consideration in assessing the effectiveness of a persuasive speech, and often this is the only class of response that we consider in evaluating speech effect. Such a concentration is not unnatu-
ral, for our first inclination is to compare intent with result. Did the
speaker succeed; was he effective; did he persuade?

Stimulation of second-level persuaders

A slightly different consequence of effective persuasion is the
transformation of listener into advocate. Occasionally a persuader
cannot make direct or effective contact with a body of persuadees,
perhaps because of an impossibility of interpersonal Associating as
we have developed that concept in Chapter 4. In such a case, the
persuader might concentrate his efforts on a smaller group of persuadees and hope that they will become persuaders to others. Elihu
Katz has written about this phenomenon as the "Two-Step Flow of
Communication."[2] He made the point that in many groups there are
persons who serve as opinion-leaders. They serve as intermediaries
between persuasive messages and others in the group.

Such an occurrence is sometimes reported in work with urban
juvenile gangs. A social worker cannot make direct contact with the
gang as a whole because the pressures against Associating are too
great. So he works to establish individual contact with the leader of
the gang, persuades that leader, and then allows the leader to serve
as his spokesman.

Modifying the image of the speaker

A persuasive speech may have still other effects upon an audience. The listener may gain impressions of the speaker which will
remain apart from the persuasive appeal. These judgments could be
important if the same speaker is heard again on another occasion.
The speaker may have demonstrated to his immediate audience the
characteristics of an expert, possessing control over the facts relat-

2. Elihu Katz, "The Two-Step Flow of Communication," in *Mass Communications*, ed.
Wilbur Schramm, 2nd ed. (Urbana: University of Illinois Press, 1960), pp. 346–365.

ing to his topic and giving evidence of considerable thought and experience. When the members of this audience see him on a future occasion, they would probably anticipate another expert treatment. And we know how much our anticipations affect our judgments.

Even within a single speech occasion this effect of the speaker's person, labeled *ethos* by the classical rhetoricians, can be influential. Once we have labeled a speaker as *expert,* or *trustworthy,* or *magnetic,* that label and all associated with it will attach to the speaker. Because first impressions are so lasting, they are extremely important. An impression formed during a speaker's introductory remarks will condition a listener for all that follows. For this reason, an unknown advocate, or an advocate of an unpopular cause, may well devote the early part of his speech to the development of his own image and only later turn to the proposition for which he is arguing. For an example of this technique in an intensely practical situation, read some of the 1952 presidential campaign speeches of Adlai Stevenson. In that campaign, Eisenhower was a national hero; while Stevenson was relatively unknown as a national figure. In the beginning of nearly every speech, Stevenson presented materials outlining his political experience and competence. Only after presenting himself did he turn to the presentation of his program.

The influence of the speaker's person has a reverse side. If a speaker lies or fabricates evidence and is found out, his possibilities for influence on any topic may be lost for a long time. It might be an interesting study, for instance, to probe the effect upon a child's image of his parents at the moment the Santa Claus myth is exploded for him.

Influence on related topics

Another side-effect of persuasion is influence upon topics or propositions beyond those discussed in the speech. Our language categories are not mutually independent. A concept that fits into one may very well fit into others. If a belief or attitude is changed toward one concept in a category, some influence of the speech may transfer to other concepts in the same or a different category, even though they are not directly related to the proposition of the persuasive speech. If the plight of the high school dropout is dramatized in an appeal for federal funds for education, the restructured concept of *dropout* may produce changes in other categories in which it occurs but which were not considered in the persuasive speech. The category *slum clearance,* for example, may be considered more favorably if a person acquired any new insights into the related problem of dropouts. In one study of persuasive speaking,[3] it was found that a speech arguing against federal government aid to health and education could have significant transfer effects to such related but unmentioned topics as federal aid to farms and federal public works programs.

Influence on thought patterns

There are yet other potential side-effects upon the listener. Not only might he experience changes in his attitudes and beliefs toward the speech proposition as well as toward other concepts; he might also have some of his strategies or patterns of thought changed. If he hears the disjunctive *either . . . or* often enough, his own patterns of thinking may tend to become two-valued, *black or white*. He may never gain, or he may lose, the ability to see subtle shades of difference or degrees along a continuum. If all the social ills in this country are continually laid at the feet of the Communists, then the label *Communist* may become so broad that it becomes synonymous with *evil* and loses specific meaning. In that condition, one could lose the ability to discriminate clearly on matters of causation. Individual patterns of causal reasoning could become oversimplified and inexact.

There are some people who hold that persuasive speaking is a neutral force. It is like a knife: it can be used as surgeon's scalpel for good or as switchblade for evil. But this position is indefensible. In persuasion, numerous effects are caused by forces other than the persuader and his specific proposition. The persuadee and the process itself contribute to the total influence. Second-level persuaders may be drawn in; related topics may be influenced; the very thought processes of the persuadee may be influenced. As was pointed out in the introduction to this chapter, apart from the specific end effect intended and sought in the persuasive speaking situations, other concomitant effects must occur. Language and language usage cannot be a neutral force.

Effects upon the speaker

We have spoken of effects upon the audience in the persuasive speaking setting. But what of the speaker? Might he also be influenced by the process? We have already commented upon feedback and the influence of listener upon speaker. If the speaker modifies his position in adapting to his listener and that modification is rewarded by listener response, it can easily be seen how the speaker's belief and attitude structures could be slightly altered by the persua-

3. Scheidel, op. cit.

sive speaking occasion. His proposition may be the same, but his emphasis may be changed. Following the speech event he may see different aspects as the more salient.

Another potential effect on a speaker is an increased commitment. A number of experimental studies have pointed to the occurrence of self-persuasion — the influence of the presentation of a speech upon the speaker himself. In one Army camp during the First World War, soldiers in a public speaking training course were to prepare speeches favorable to Army life. It was found that, as a result, some "chronic kickers" showed marked improvement in morale.[4] In other Army studies, it was found that the phonetic alphabet was more easily learned if the listeners were required to rehearse aloud rather than simply listen to a filmstrip, and group discussion, involving active participation by all in the group, was found to be more influential than a lecture in which the group listened to one speaker. John Dewey taught that we learn by doing, and many educational procedures are based on this principle. By actively playing a role, one becomes a changed person.

From our description of the persuasive process, we can see a number of explanations for self-persuasion by a speaker. As a speaker invents his arguments and presents them, he provides a special focus; the categories he employs receive greater prominence or salience in his thinking. The experience of speaking the ideas may be rewarding, which in turn would help his learning of the ideas. The audience may approve and respond favorably, or the speaker may reward his own act in terms of self-esteem. By demonstrating to himself a degree of mastery in a public speaking situation, he may fulfill a need.

We can see, then, that the potential consequences of persuasive speaking are many. The listener can experience changes in his position on the speech proposition, or on remotely related propositions, or even in his habits and patterns of manipulating categories, his strategies of thought. The speaker may experience changes in his position and in his degree of commitment to that position. All these changes are possible, and they should be carefully assessed as a first step in any analysis of a persuasive speaking event. A determination of the total effect of any speech requires full, intensive, and accurate description of its circumstances and results.

It is important that we see how wide the range of persuasive influences is, for we shall want to consider the total possible effects as we turn to questions of ethics, or the evaluation of the effects achieved by persuasion.

4. For additional details on this and related studies see chapter on "Acquiring Conviction Through Active Participation," in Hovland, Janis, and Kelley, op. cit.

ETHICAL CONSIDERATIONS

The ethics of persuasion is at once a fascinating and yet a most perplexing topic. It has caused difficulties for most writers on persuasion. Many authors seem torn between what they believe *is* and what they believe *ought to be* and are unable to bring these two views into a harmonious relationship. They write of man's behavior as emotional-rational but frequently insist that the evaluation of that behavior be solely rational. They often seem to focus too narrowly upon the speaker, neglecting the contribution of the listener in the process, and upon the consequences bearing on the speech proposition, neglecting the many side-effects of persuasion. We will discuss here two of the prominent issues in the ethics of persuasion and then suggest a few guiding principles.

Do ends justify means?

The answer often given to this question is "no." The usual supporting argument is that even if the end is beneficial for "the masses," we cannot accept some techniques (those labeled *unethical*) for supporting it. This approach distinctly separates ends and means and holds that both of them must be evaluated.

On the other hand, it is possible to answer this question with a qualified "yes." This does not mean, of course, that any end justifies any means. But one could maintain that the ends ought to justify the means, for it is difficult to think of anything else that does. Sometimes means are considered to justify themselves: "Virtue is its own reward." But the word *reward* implies action and consequences. It is the consequences of the action of virtue which justifies virtue.

Much of the difficulty concerning this question arises from the fact that *ends* and *means*, as categories, are not easily separated. In general, the ends-means dichotomy depends upon our assumptions about cause and effect relations. If X is followed by Y at a high level of probability, we might say that X is the cause of Y or the means to the end Y. Thus, if one performs X, he has also performed Y; and if he wants to perform Y, he may have to perform X. The two are really consequents of one decision on the part of the agent and thus should be regarded coordinately rather than in some sort of hierarchical or sequential relation to one another. It has been truly said that "In the means, the end is already performed."

Perhaps a definition here will eliminate much of the problem and clarify the present position. When some persons speak of ends, they refer only to the speaker's *intentions*. But, as stated above, intentions are private, covert, difficult or impossible to measure and evaluate. The old plantation expression was "'Mean to' don't pick no cotton." The view here is that ends should be considered as *consequences* or results. The total consequences of a persuasive speaking occasion, the side-effects as well as the direct effects, the long-range results as well as the immediate results, should be the elements judged. Intentions and actions are on such different levels that they are not easily related. Actions are specific, observable, and well bounded in time. Intentions are not so exact, cannot be precisely shared or sensed by another, and may well change over time. From the view of ends as *intentions*, the question of ends and means is inexact. When ends are considered as *consequences*, the matter is clarified. The standard becomes: Do the total consequences of this speech justify its having been given, as it was given?

What absolute standards apply?

In writings on the ethics of persuasion, a few absolute standards are often given, such as:

1. It is unethical to falsify or fabricate.
2. It is unethical to distort so that a piece of evidence does not convey its true intent.
3. It is unethical to make conscious use of specious reasoning.
4. It is unethical to deceive the audience about the speaker's intent.[5]

Or, for example:

1. It is, of course, unethical for a speaker to distort or falsify evidence.
2. It is unethical for a speaker to use emotional appeals when he lacks evidence to support them, or when he knows his listeners would not support his conclusion if they had the time and opportunity to investigate the problem for themselves.
3. It is unethical for a speaker to divert attention from weaknesses in his argument by unsupported attacks on his opponent or by appeals to hatred, intolerance, bigotry, and fear.
4. It is unethical for a speaker to conceal his real purpose, or the organization he represents, pretending to speak objectively when he is an advocate of one point of view.

5. Wayne C. Minnick, *The Art of Persuasion* (Boston: Houghton Mifflin Company, 1957), p. 284.

5. It is unethical for a speaker to pose as an "authority" when he has only a layman's knowledge of the subject.[6]

But are there certain means of persuasion that are absolutely wrong and that must never be employed? Can we accept the injunction that one should never lie? Consider an everyday family situation. Parents sometimes tell their children "I don't think so," when in fact they do think so, but, not being sure, they choose not to allow the children to be disappointed. If the parents say yes and are wrong, the children will be greatly disappointed in the outcome of the event as well as in the parents' judgment. The parents can prevent possible disappointment by saying no. But if the event does occur, the children will be unsure of parental judgment even though pleased with the event. If the event does not occur, they will be unhappy but prepared for it. We are very often faced with decisions similar to this. In many such cases, making a statement of fact when one is not actually possible is not necessarily wrong but may be justified by the ends or consequences. You may ask, why not tell the absolute truth? Tell the children that you aren't sure. The practical answer is, wait until you have children and try it. Childhood and indecision seem incompatible.

For the sake of morale, a nation at war often does not disclose the full measure of its losses to its citizens and may overemphasize the damage inflicted upon the enemy. Combatants' accounts of losses in any battle rarely agree. Even without outright lying, a certain emphasis may be deceiving; for example, more time may be spent discussing the battle won than the battle lost. The overriding necessity of morale for national survival may justify such practices. The suggestion here is that certain consequences may justify means that would not be justified by other consequences; in addition, certain consequences of persuasive messages are imaginable that would justify almost any available means of persuasion.

But to understand this point correctly, one must consider what we mean by the word *justify*. To say that a lie is "justified" does not say that the lie, *as such*, is "good." It only implies that the matter is one of balance. If one had to choose between telling the truth or telling a lie and saving a life, he might hold that the positive consequences of saving the life outweigh the negative consequences of telling a lie. In such a case, the lie might be said to be justified.

The point is that most human decisions are made on balance. We must weigh potential positive and negative consequences. We face the conflict of desiring candy and at the same time desiring good teeth. We want high grades, but we want leisure time. There are no

6. Henry L. Ewbank and J. Jeffery Auer, *Discussion and Debate*, 2nd ed. (New York: Appleton-Century-Crofts, Inc., 1951), p. 258.

easy solutions. And once a decision is made, all the negative as well as all the positive consequences must be accepted. We began this chapter by pointing out the conflict inherent in the essence of communication. Communication creates "humanness" but at the same time necessarily involves manipulation.

Apart from our question of whether some means of persuasion should never be employed, a more general question arises. Should we accept the presentation of any absolute prescriptions for behavior? Can we accept the absolutes that one should never lie or that one should always refrain from the use of highly emotionalized language appeals which do not prompt reasoned consideration? In the first place, we see many exceptions to these dicta. Consider the example above of a nation at war. In the future, national leaders doubtless will continue to withhold the truth and even lie if they believe that the truth might shatter morale and create chaos. From the view presented here, this action might be justifiable.

Plato probably advocated the cause of truth as strongly as anyone. In the *Phaedrus* he urges that a speaker should know and speak the truth. And we all know how he took the Sophists to task for substituting appearances for truth and holding that "man is the measure of all things." Yet in his ideal society of the *Republic*, even Plato recognized the possible need for lying.

> Then if any one at all is to have the privilege of lying, the rulers of the State should be the persons; and they, in their dealings either with enemies or with their own citizens, may be allowed to lie for the public good. But nobody else should meddle with anything of the kind. . . .[7]

A hundred years ago the English parliamentarian and writer John Morley wrote a work *On Compromise,* in which he argued persuasively against the practice of ever misleading anyone. He discusses a case of an intellectual who does not believe in hell but who uses it as a fiction for his children and servants. The difficulty Morley sees is that:

> . . . in making false notions the proofs or close associates of true ones, you are exposing the latter to the ruin which awaits the former. For example, if you have in the minds of children or servants associated honesty, industry, truthfulness, with the fear of hell-fire, then supposing this fear to become extinct in their

7. Plato, op. cit., p. 651.

minds, — which, being unfounded in truth, it is in constant risk of doing, — the virtues associated with it are likely to be weakened exactly in proportion as that association was strong.[8]

Although we do not here accept Morley's view as an absolute, his position is most compelling and should be considered.

Tact is a label we use as a euphemism for the lies we tell every day. Sometimes it is convenient to call them *half-truths*, *little white lies*, or *slight distortions*. Whatever the label, are these lies absolutely harmful in their consequences? H. L. Mencken wrote as his own epitaph:

If, after I depart this vale, you ever remember me and have thought to please my ghost, forgive some sinner and wink your eye at some homely girl.

That wink may be a lie, but a wonderful one. And so the first reason for not advocating absolute prescriptions for behavior is that we may have to allow, and even advocate, exceptions. When we allow exceptions, an absolute is no longer.

Another reason for opposing a list of absolute standards is the difficulty of interpreting them. What one swears is truth, another swears is lie. How are we to know? As William James wrote in his essay, "The Will to Believe":

But if we are empiricists, if we believe that no bell in us tolls to let us know for certain when truth is in our grasp, then it seems a piece of idle fantasticality to preach so solemnly our duty of waiting for the bell.[9]

From what we have said about language categories, we know that the category of *truth* itself cannot have identical meaning for any two persons. It is nearly as generalized and indefinite as *good*.

Consider the passages below. Which is the more emotional, immoderate statement? Which calls less for reasoned consideration?

Hitler is a monster of wickedness, insatiable in his lust for blood and plunder. Not content with having all Europe under his heel or else terrorized into various forms of abject submission, he must now carry his work of butchery and desolation among the

---

8. John Morley, "Of the Possible Utility of Error," in *Representative Essays in Modern Thought*, ed. Harrison Steeves and Frank Ristine (New York: American Book Company, 1913), p. 151.

9. William James, "The Will to Believe," in Steeves and Ristine, op. cit., p. 96.

vast multitudes of Russia and of Asia. This terrible military machine . . . must be in continual motion, grinding up human lives and trampling down the homes and the rights of hundreds of millions of men.

Moreover, it must be fed not only with flesh but with oil. So now this bloodthirsty guttersnipe must launch his mechanized armies upon new fields of slaughter, pillage, and devastation. Poor as are the Russian peasants, workmen and soldiers, he must steal from them their daily bread. He must devour their harvests. . . .

I also see the dull, drilled, docile, brutish masses of the Hun soldiery, plodding on like a swarm of crawling locusts.

Even my warnings against night bombings of the civilian population, as advocated by Mr. Churchill, were interpreted as a sign of German impotence. He, the most bloodthirsty or amateurish strategist that history has ever known, actually saw fit to believe that the reserve displayed for months by the German Air Force could be looked upon only as proof of their incapacity to fly by night. . . .

That these warnings failed to impress Mr. Churchill does not surprise me in the least. For what does this man care for the lives of others? What does he care for culture or for architecture? . . .

The appeal to forsake me, made to the German nation by this fool and his satellites on May Day, of all days, is only to be explained either as symptomatic of a paralytic disease or of a drunkard's ravings. His abnormal state of mind also gave birth to a decision to transform the Balkans into a theatre of war. For over five years this man has been chasing around Europe like a madman in search of something he could set on fire. . . .

God knows that I wanted peace.[10]

Do we censure Churchill on Hitler, Hitler on Churchill, both, or neither? Perhaps each of these men believed what he said. Apart from the ideas expressed, it is difficult to consistently censure one and not the other for his use of emotional language.

The final and major objection to a list of absolute prescriptions has to do with the nature of the absolute. The absolute is just that. It is assertive and allows for no exceptions. If we do find occasional exceptions, then the absolute is lost, and we have nothing remaining. The difficulty is that we have learned the dogma given us without necessarily learning why. We have the absolute prescription but no reason for it. It would seem much better that we be guided by princi-

10. *The World's Great Speeches*, pp. 476–477 and 507–509.

ples based on reasons rather than by prescriptions for behavior based on decree. Exceptions do not destroy principles, and principles are more flexible for application in varying contexts.

Guiding principles

What principles could be suggested for evaluating persuasive speaking influence? First, we would maintain that responsibility for consequences, and any assessment of praise or blame, fall equally upon speaker and listener. Persuasion has been described as a process which unites persuader and persuadee, a process in which both must contribute to the total outcome and in which both are influenced. Although the speaker may exercise a choice in speaking, the listener may also exercise a choice in listening. Some may say that an audience was unschooled, ignorant, misled, and that its members couldn't help their actions because they had no real choice. But what of the speaker? He also could be unschooled, ignorant, misled, and have had no real choice.

Unless we believe that a speaker can "know" absolutely, it is unreasonable to expect him to serve as his sole monitor; to serve as his own and his only check. Such an expectation would be contrary to human nature. It would ask a man to be able to consider himself as *object*, to see himself without bias as observer. We cannot observe anything in that manner—let alone ourselves. It seems more reasonable to lay some of the responsibility for any checking behavior upon the listener. He is at least in a better position to do this than is the speaker. The fact remains that any act of persuasion requires the active participation of both persuader and persuadee. It seems preferable that they share the responsibilities for the act.

We would say that there is one general principle for evaluating any persuasive influence. The principle is that *every party in the persuasive speaking process, persuader or persuadee, must bear the full responsibilities for the full consequences of his actions.* The possible range of consequences following from persuasion were outlined earlier in this chapter. Any and all of these influences would be the responsibility of the parties to the persuasion.

Our primary interest here, however, is not to find someone at whose feet can be laid the responsibilities for the consequences of any persuasive act. It would be better to present some guides that may be helpful for any potential persuader. We would first hold that it is the duty of the speaker (and to his advantage) to consider and weigh all possible and probable consequences of his speaking. He must consider the potential effects of the manner as well as the matter of his persuasion. He will be held accountable. If the speaker does not lie, it is preferable that he do this as a matter of choice rather than as following an absolute.

In the controversy concerning freedom of speech, it has been stated that a person does not have the right to step into a crowded theatre and scream "fire." If he does so, he may be punished for the act. But imagine that there is a fire. The case becomes more interesting. Perhaps then our subject may scream "fire" and be absolved of any legal liability. In this latter case however, he may be liable to moral censure. If his scream has the consequences of starting a panic and mad trampling when another act may have promoted a calmer exit, then his choice was a bad one. He is in part responsible for these consequences, and he should be censured for it. If a government leader can maintain morale by means other than lying about battle losses, perhaps he should do so, for the risk of unfavorable consequences if the truth comes out will be greatly reduced. Perhaps if the advertiser could emphasize the merits of his product and rely less on colorful and noisy trappings, all advertising might be taken more seriously. Any persuadee can become surfeited to spectacle.

Let us conclude on a positive note. All of the positions presented here concerning ethics place a heavy burden upon any persuader. He might ask if it would be safer not to persuade at all. The answer is yes, and this is probably why many go through life without creating disturbances, getting involved, or attempting to stir anyone. But the decision not to persuade *is a decision,* and one must be held accountable for it. If one could have persuaded and chooses not to, or simply does not, then he is just as responsible for his action as another whose decision to attempt to persuade led to unhappy consequences. William James closes his essay "The Will to Believe" with the thought:

> We stand on a mountain pass in the midst of whirling snow and blinding mist, through which we get glimpses now and then of paths which may be deceptive. If we stand still, we shall be frozen to death. If we take the wrong road, we shall be dashed to pieces. We do not certainly know whether there is any right one. What must we do? "Be strong and of a good courage." Act for the best, hope for the best, and take what comes.[11]

Again as Plato reports the last words of Socrates:

> When my sons are grown up, I would ask you, O my friends, to punish them; and I would have you trouble them, as I have

11. James, op. cit., p. 97.

troubled you, if they seem to care about riches, or anything, more than about virtue; or if they pretend to be something when they are really nothing, — then reprove them, as I have reproved you, for not caring about that for which they ought to care, and thinking that they are something when they are really nothing. And if you do this, both I and my sons will have received justice at your hands.[12]

Persuasive speaking can be a mighty force, and one must always be sensitive to those occasions in which an attempt at persuasion is a duty.

12. Plato, op. cit., p. 423.

MATERIALS FOR ANALYSIS, DELIBERATION, AND DISCUSSION

The following materials are included to serve two purposes: (1) to give guided practice in the analysis of persuasive materials and (2) to help integrate the concepts and principles developed in this book. The first aim is rather easily achieved. It asks the reader to apply the terms and concepts of this work to real instances of persuasion. The principles developed here should then become clearer, and the reader's future analysis of any persuasive message should be more complete. The second goal is more difficult to achieve. It asks the reader to relate concepts with one another, to bring materials from different parts of the book together. The reader is asked, for example, to relate our value systems with our reasoning processes, to employ classical concepts in contemporary analysis, to combine processes which have been developed individually so that they may jointly serve to explain persuasive influence.

THE GETTYSBURG ADDRESS AND THE BROWN WRAPPING PAPER

Speech as a Process

At one time or another most of us have heard that popular romantic tale of how Lincoln prepared the Gettysburg Address. One account describes the writing of the Address during the train trip from Washington to Gettysburg:

> . . . the people had a right to the best he could give, and he would give them his best; at least he could see to it that the words were real and were short; at least he would not, so, exhaust their patience. And the work might as well be done now in the leisure of the journey. He put a hand, big, power-

ful, labor-knotted, into first one sagging pocket and then another, in search of a pencil, and drew out one broken across the end. He glanced about inquiringly – there was nothing to write upon. Across the car the Secretary of State had just opened a package of books and their wrapping of brown paper lay on the floor, torn carelessly in a zig-zag. The president stretched a long arm. "Mr. Seward, may I have this to do a little writing?" he asked, and the Secretary protested, insisting on finding better material.

But Lincoln, with few words, had his way, and soon the untidy stump of a pencil was at work and the great head, the deep-lined face, bent over Seward's bit of brown paper, the whole man absorbed in his task.[1]

The best historical evidence gives little support to the above account. It seems that the author, Mary Raymond Shipman Andrews, got her information from her son Paul Shipman Andrews, who got it from Walter Burlingame, who got it from Anson Burlingame, who reportedly got it from Edward Everett. It is most likely that Lincoln labored on the Gettysburg Address off and on for a few weeks before the dedication as well as in Gettysburg the evening prior to the ceremony. Doubtless he continued polishing his language and perhaps even added some previously unplanned wording during the moments of utterance, as would any skilled speaker. But the speech reflected weeks rather than hours of preparation. Even the specific thoughts and wording were developed over a longer period of time. Compare the Address given on November 19, 1863, with the following excerpts from informal remarks presented *four months earlier* – July 7, 1863.

> How long ago is it? – eighty-odd years since, on the Fourth of July for the first time in the history of the world a nation by its representatives, assembled and declared as a self-evident truth, that "all men are created equal." . . . and now, on this last Fourth of July just passed, when we have a gigantic Rebellion, at the bottom of which is an effort to overthrow the principle that all men are created equal. . . . Gentlemen, this is a glorious theme, and the occasion for a speech; but I am not prepared to make one worthy of the occasion.[2]

1. Mary Raymond Shipman Andrews, *The Perfect Tribute* (New York: Charles Scribner's Sons, 1923), pp. 5–6. If interested, see David C. Mearns, "Unknown at This Address," in *Lincoln and the Gettysburg Address*, ed. Allan Nevins (Urbana: University of Illinois Press, 1964).
2. *The Collected Works of Abraham Lincoln*, ed. Roy P. Basler (New Brunswick, N.J.: Rutgers University Press, 1953), VI, pp. 319–320.

On November 19, 1863, Lincoln again drew upon this "glorious theme" and he was prepared to make a speech worthy of the occasion.

We ought to do all that we can to stamp out this old myth that the Gettysburg Address was created by Lincoln in a few hours using a broken pencil and scraps of brown wrapping paper while bouncing along on a clattering train. This is an especially harmful fiction to perpetrate in the primary grades, for it may lead students to believe something of value can be created without any considerable effort. Also, this story violates the spirit of our conception of speech as a process, as an ongoing dynamic phenomenon with antecedents stretching back in time.

Questions

1. What is lost when one views a speech without taking its development and context into consideration? You might wish to read Lincoln's Cooper Union Address of 1860 in connection with this question. Lincoln put great effort into the preparation of that address and one cannot read it without being impressed by the time which must have been required to do the necessary research.

2. What is important in the distinction between *general preparation* and *specific preparation* for a speech event?

FRANCIS BACON'S "IDOLS OF THE MIND"

Potential Fallacies in Man's Thinking

The following excerpts are taken from the *Novum Organum* by the English philosopher Francis Bacon (1561–1626).[3] Bacon was attempting here to classify and analyze the idols, or false notions, or fallacies inherent in our reasoning. The language is a bit difficult but try to read over the items quickly and see whether you can "complete" the meaning. Can you fit some of your own categories to Bacon's thoughts? The items have been renumbered for easier reference.

> A. IDOLS OF THE TRIBE
> The idols of the tribe are inherent in human nature and the very tribe or race of man; for man's sense is falsely asserted to be the standard of things; on the contrary, all the perceptions both of the senses and the mind bear reference to man and not to the universe, and the human mind resembles those uneven mirrors which impart their own properties to

---

3. Francis Bacon, *Advancement of Learning* and *Novum Organum,* special introduction by James E. Creighton (New York: The Colonial Press, 1900), pp. 319–326.

different objects, from which rays are emitted and distort and disfigure them.

1. The human understanding, from its peculiar nature, easily supposes a greater degree of order and equality in things than it really finds; and although many things in nature be *sui generis* [singular] and most irregular, will yet invent parallels and conjugates and relatives, where no such thing is. Hence the fiction, that all celestial bodies move in perfect circles. . . .

2. The human understanding, when any proposition has been once laid down (either from general admission and belief, or from the pleasure it affords), forces everything else to add fresh support and confirmation. . . .

3. The human understanding is most excited by that which strikes and enters the mind at once and suddenly, and by which the imagination is immediately filled and inflated. It then begins almost imperceptibly to conceive and suppose that everything is similar to the few objects which have taken possession of the mind. . . .

4. The human understanding is active and cannot halt or rest, but even, though without effect, still presses forward. Thus we cannot conceive of any end or external boundary of the world. . . .

5. . . . man always believes more readily that which he prefers . . . his feelings imbue and corrupt his understanding in innumerable and sometimes imperceptible ways.

6. But by far the greatest impediment and aberration of the human understanding proceeds from the dullness, incompetency, and errors of the senses; since whatever strikes the senses preponderates over everything. . . .

7. The human understanding is, by its own nature, prone to abstraction, and supposes that which is fluctuating to be fixed.

B. IDOLS OF THE CAVE OR DEN

. . . everybody has his own individual den or cavern, which intercepts and corrupts the light of nature, either from his own peculiar and singular disposition, or from his education and intercourse with others, or from his reading. . . . Heraclitus said well that men search for knowledge in lesser worlds, and not in the greater or common world.

1. Some men become attached to particular sciences and contemplations, either from supposing themselves the authors and inventors of them, or from having bestowed the

greatest pains upon such subjects, and thus become most habituated to them.

2. The greatest and, perhaps, radical distinction between different men's dispositions for philosophy and the sciences is this, that some are more vigorous and active in observing the differences of things, others in observing their resemblances. . . .

3. Some dispositions evince an unbounded admiration of antiquity, others eagerly embrace novelty. . . .

4. The contemplation of nature and of bodies in their individual form distracts and weakens the understanding; but the contemplation of nature and of bodies in their general composition and formation stupefies and relaxes it.

C. IDOLS OF THE MARKET-PLACE

There are also idols formed by the reciprocal intercourse and society of man with man, . . . from the commerce and association of men with each other; for men converse by means of language, but words are formed at the will of the generality, and there arises from a bad and unapt formation of words a wonderful [powerful] obstruction to the mind.

1. . . . men imagine that their reason governs words, whilst, in fact, words react upon the understanding. . . .

2. Words are generally formed in a popular sense, and define things by those broad lines which are most obvious to the vulgar mind.

3. The idols imposed upon the understanding by words are of two kinds. They are either the names of things which have no existence, . . . or they are the names of actual objects, but confused, badly defined, and hastily and irregularly abstracted from things. Fortune, the *primum mobile,* the planetary orbits, the element of fire, and the like fictions, which owe their birth to futile and false theories, are instances of the first kind. . . . One of the least faulty classes is that of the names of substances, particularly of the less abstract and more defined species; . . . words signifying actions are more faulty, as to generate, to corrupt, to change; but the most faulty are those denoting qualities, . . . as heavy, light, rare, dense.

D. IDOLS OF THE THEATRE

Lastly, there are idols which have crept into men's minds from the various dogmas of peculiar systems of philosophy, and also from the perverted rules of demonstration . . . for we regard all the systems of philosophy hitherto received or imagined as so many plays brought out and performed, creating fictitious and theatrical worlds. . . . Nor, again, do we allude merely to general systems, but also to many elements and axioms of sciences which have become inveterate by tradition, implicit credence, and neglect.

1. The idols of the theatre are not innate, nor do they introduce themselves secretly into the understanding, but they are manifestly instilled and cherished by the fictions of theories and depraved rules of demonstration. . . . In general, men take for the groundwork of their philosophy either too much from a few topics, or too little from many; in either case their philosophy is founded on too narrow a basis of experiment and natural history, and decides on too scanty grounds.

Questions

1. Bacon wrote, "The syllogism consists of propositions, propositions of words; words are the signs of notions. If, therefore, the notions (which form the basis of the whole) be confused and carelessly abstracted from things, there is no solidity in the superstructure." What comparisons can be drawn between this statement and our treatment of categories and language in Chapter 2?

2. Every one of Bacon's idols seems to apply (directly or indirectly) to our treatment of human behavior. Can you take the excerpts 'above and find parallel concerns and relationships in Chapter 2?

3. To which process—Receiving, Focusing, Associating, or Resolving—do the "Idols of the Tribe" relate most closely?

4. How will "Idols of the Cave" influence the process of Focusing?—The process of Associating?

5. What can a speaker do to minimize the potential negative effects of the "Idols of the Market Place"? What can the listener do?

6. To what extent may our value systems be "Idols of the Theatre"?

7. Could we profitably conceive of Bacon's "Idols" as *topoi* for the invention process in speech development?

MARTIN LUTHER KING, JR.

Speech Arrangement

In a sermon by Martin Luther King, Jr., titled "The Dimensions of a Complete Life," the following organizational pattern was used.[4] King argued that all three dimensions were necessary for a complete life.

4. From a tape recording of the sermon.

A. The Length of Life

(King here spoke not of longevity, but rather of the "push of a life forward" to achieve ambitions and personal ends — man's attempt to become what he is capable of being; self-actualization.)

B. The Breadth of Life

(King discussed the "outward concern for welfare of others" — the broader concern for all of humanity.)

C. The Height of Life

(King spoke of man's "upward reach for God" — his concern for a power above man.)

Questions

1. How would King's organizational pattern help prevent filtering?
2. The use of the three physical dimensions probably contributes to clarity and to emphasis of the main ideas. How would these effects be explained in terms of the concepts developed in Chapter 4?
3. How does this pattern achieve unity and completeness in the speech?

BARTOLOMEO VANZETTI

Eloquence and Speech Effectiveness

We have listed as major qualities of style: correctness, clarity, appropriateness, embellishment. What are the components of eloquence?

A robbery and the murder of a paymaster and guard in South Braintree, Massachusetts, on April 15, 1920, aroused world-wide attention when Nicola Sacco and Bartolomeo Vanzetti, two Italian immigrants, were convicted of the crime and executed on August 22, 1927. The proceedings brought out the facts that the men were draft-dodgers, atheists, and philosophical anarchists. The nature of the evidence, the character of the judge, and the demeanor of the men themselves made many around the world believe that the men were not involved in the robbery at all but were convicted only because they held unpopular and antisocial views. The following statement, made by Bartolomeo Vanzetti a few months before his execution, is considered by some to be eloquent.

> If it had not been for these thing, I might have live out my life talking at street corners to scorning men. I might have die, unmarked, unknown, a failure. Now we are not a failure. This is our career and our triumph. Never in our full life

could we hope to do such work for tolerance, for joostice, for man's understanding of man as now we do by accident. Our words — our lives — lives of a good shoemaker and a poor fish-peddler — all! That last moment belongs to us — that agony is our triumph.[5]

Questions

1. Vanzetti's statement does not seem to be especially correct, clear, appropriate, or embellished. How could it have any influential effect? Does the fact that these men are to die make this speech eloquent, or could completing and Associating account for some of the persuasive effect?

2. In what ways could we *identify* with this man who is so unlike ourselves?

3. In Chapter 5, six different possible consequences of persuasive speaking were presented. Try to explain Vanzetti's total effect in the light of these six possible consequences. For example, to what degree did Vanzetti's statement enlist second-level persuaders?

4. To what degree would you expect the effect of Vanzetti's statement to be related to changes in belief and/or affect? In what ways might the "meaning" of the persuasive proposition, or the "object" of judgment, have been changed for the listener?

5. Try to explain Vanzetti's effectiveness in terms of Aristotle's "modes of persuasion" presented in Chapter 1. Do the same for the positions listed under the sections "Modern Speech Approaches" and "Modern Psychological Approaches," also in Chapter 1. Compare and contrast these explanations with one another and with an explanation based upon the principles developed in this book.

LINCOLN'S FIRST INAUGURAL

Speech Style

Effectiveness in the use of language is not easily amenable to close and objective analysis. Consider the following paragraph suggested by William H. Seward as a conclusion for Lincoln's First Inaugural Address.

> I close. We are not, we must not be, aliens or enemies, but fellow-countrymen and brethren. Although passion has strained our bonds of affection too hardly, they must not, I am sure they will not, be broken. The mystic chords which, proceeding from so many battlefields and so many patriot graves, pass through all the hearts and all the hearths in this broad continent of ours, will yet again harmonize in their

5. Osmond K. Fraenkel, *The Sacco-Vanzetti Case* (New York: Alfred A. Knopf, Inc., 1931), p. 21.

ancient music when breathed upon by the guardian angel of the nation.[6]

In his revision, suggesting among other things that it is possible for a political figure to have more to offer than a ghost writer, Lincoln closed with:

> I am loath to close. We are not enemies, but friends. We must not be enemies. Though passion may have strained, it must not break our bonds of affection. The mystic chords of memory, stretching from every battlefield, and patriot grave, to every living heart and hearthstone, all over this broad land, will yet swell the chorus of the Union, when again touched, as surely they will be, by the better angels of our nature.

Question

1. Compare Seward's and Lincoln's alternative conclusions for Lincoln's Address word for word, phrase for phrase. How do you account for the fact that Lincoln's is the better?

LINCOLN'S LETTERS

Differences in Persuasion

Lincoln's speeches and letters provide a number of models of excellence in the use of language which would be fully appropriate even in our day. Consider the following well-known letters representing widely differing purposes, audiences, and approaches.

Executive Mansion, Washington
February 3, 1862

Major General McClellan:
My dear Sir:
You and I have distinct and different plans for a movement of the Army of the Potomac—yours to be down the Chesapeake up the Rappahannock to Urbana, and across land to the terminus of the railroad on the York River—, mine to

---

6. Seward's suggested passage, and Lincoln's, which follows, are from *Abraham Lincoln: His Speeches and Writings*, ed. Roy P. Basler (Cleveland: The World Publishing Company, 1946), p. 48. If interested, see Basler's essay "Lincoln's Development as a Writer," in the same volume, pp. 1–49.

move directly to a point on the Railroad South West of Manassas.

If you will give me satisfactory answers to the following questions, I shall gladly yield my plan to yours.

1st. Does not your plan involve a greatly larger expenditure of time and money than mine?

2nd. Wherein is a victory *more certain* by your plan than mine?

3rd. Wherein is a victory *more valuable* by your plan than mine?

4th. In fact, would it not be *less* valuable in this, that it would break no great line of the enemie's communications, while mine would?

5th. In case of disaster, would not a safe retreat be more difficult by your plan than mine?

Yours truly,
A. Lincoln[7]

Executive Mansion
Washington, Nov. 21, 1864

To Mrs. Bixby, Boston, Mass.

Dear Madam, —

I have been shown in the files of the War Department a statement of the Adjutant General of Massachusetts, that you are the mother of five sons who have died gloriously on the field of battle.

I feel how weak and fruitless must be any words of mine which should attempt to beguile you from the grief of a loss so overwhelming. But I cannot refrain from tendering you the consolation that may be found in the thanks of the Republic they died to save.

I pray that our Heavenly Father may assuage the anguish of your bereavement, and leave you only the cherished memory of the loved and lost, and the solemn pride that must be yours, to have laid so costly a sacrifice upon the altar of freedom.

Yours, very sincerely and respectfully.
A. Lincoln[8]

7. *The Collected Works of Abraham Lincoln,* V, pp. 118–119.
8. Ibid., VIII, pp. 116–117.

Questions

1. Is one letter less "persuasive" in intent than the other? To what degree does each ask for belief and/or affect change?

2. Why is there a difference in organizational pattern in these letters? What are the differing purposes served?

3. Analyze each message in terms of how well it treats the "status of the question."

4. What ends are served by the use of questions in the letter to McClellan? Can a question be persuasive? Is Lincoln providing special *topoi* for McClellan? Is it possible to relate the questioning technique to Focusing?

A STUDENT'S CONTEST SPEECH

Ethos

The following excerpts are taken from a short speech composed and delivered in 1955 by a college student, Ralph Zimmermann.[9] Mr. Zimmermann won first place in the Interstate Oratorical Association contest with the speech. The excerpts begin with his introduction.

> I am a hemophiliac. To many of you, that word signifies little or nothing. A few may pause a moment and then remember that it has something to do with bleeding. Probably none of you can appreciate the gigantic impact of what those words mean to me. . . .
>
> What does it really mean to be a hemophiliac? The first indication comes in early childhood when a small scratch may bleed for hours. By the time the hemophiliac reaches school age, he begins to suffer from internal bleeding into muscles, joints, the stomach, the kidneys. This latter type is far more serious, for external wounds can usually be stopped in minutes with topical thromboplastin or a pressure bandage. But internal bleeding can be checked only by changes in the blood by means of transfusion or plasma injections. If internal bleeding into a muscle or joint goes unchecked repeatedly, muscle contraction and bone deformity inevitably result. My crooked left arm, the built-up heel on my right shoe, and the full-length brace on my left leg offer mute but undeniable testimony to that fact. . . .

9. Excerpts taken from the text of the speech, "Mingled Blood," by Ralph Zimmermann, in Carroll C. Arnold, Douglas Ehninger, and John C. Gerber, *The Speaker's Resource Book* (Glenview, Ill.: Scott, Foresman and Company, 1966), pp. 98–100. Reprinted by permission of the Interstate Oratorical Association.

You might ask—but what can I do? What do you expect of me? The answer lies in the title of this oration: mingled blood. For all that boy needs is blood, blood, and more blood. Blood for transfusions, blood for fresh frozen plasma, blood for serum fractions. Not Red Cross Bank Blood, for stored blood loses its clot-producing factors. But fresh blood directly from you to him in a matter of hours. . . .

I cannot change that part of my life which is past. I cannot change my hemophilia. Therefore, I must ask you to help those hemophiliacs that need help. For I remember too well my older brother Herbert, so shattered in adolescence by hemophilia, that his tombstone reads like a blessing: "May 10, 1927—April 6, 1950, Thy Will Be Done." And I ask you to help hemophiliacs because one day my grandson may need your blood. . . .

Questions

1. How has the speaker made use of *ethos*? What factors of ethos are stressed? Can you "appreciate the impact" of hemophilia upon the speaker? Do you *identify* with him? What "associations" come to mind?

2. What other "modes of persuasion" are employed in these quoted portions of the speech? How are they developed?

3. What is your judgment of the ethics of such use of personal proof and appeal in a college speaking contest? Could the setting influence a judgment of ethics? What were the potential consequences of this speech? What were the possible audience reactions?

THE HAROLD E. STASSEN-THOMAS E. DEWEY DEBATE OF 1948

Invention and the Process of Persuasion

In 1948, Harold E. Stassen, former Governor of Minnesota, and Thomas E. Dewey, Governor of New York, were contending for the Republican presidential nomination. On May 17, in Portland, Oregon, they met in a radio debate on the proposition—Resolved: that the Communist party in the United States should be outlawed. Stassen upheld the affirmative position and Dewey argued the negative. Below are a few excerpts from that debate.[10]

STASSEN:

(S1) During the recent war I saw many young Americans killed. I watched ships explode and burn, planes crash in

10. From a tape recording of the debate broadcast by radio from Portland, Oregon.

flames, men, our men, my friends, fall. . . . In the midst of these experiences I thought more deeply than ever before of the way in which men should live, of the preciousness of freedom, of the future of America.

(S2) Such a law is constitutional under Article 4 Section 4 of the United States Constitution. A very eminent lawyer, the honorable William L. Ransom, past president of the American Bar Association, agrees on its constitutionality in an able article in *The American Law Journal* this month. The language of the Supreme Court of the United States in the case of Ohio vs. Akron indicates that the Supreme Court would uphold its constitutionality.

(S3) I am not certain of the reasons for Mr. Henry Wallace's opposition to my position, but I am confident that Governor Dewey's opposition is completely sincere. But I respectfully ask him to reconsider his opposition as I believe he is mistaken.

(S4) In each of the other countries – Poland, Hungary, Yugoslavia, Romania, Bulgaria, Albania, and finally Czechoslovakia – the Communists used the blessing of legality as an aid to organizing an underground movement, and finally betrayed the liberties of the people – brought them under the domination of the Kremlin in Moscow.

DEWEY:

(D1) Now I find that the difficulty here tonight is that Mr. Stassen has not adhered to his subject or his statements. He says he is for the Mundt bill because, says Mr. Stassen, it outlaws the Communist party. But the fact of the matter is, he is in grievous error. The only authority he quotes is the head of the Communist party, which is not exactly a very good authority when seeking the truth.

(D2) Now, I suppose, if you say, "Let's outlaw the Communist party and preserve our liberties," and if you say it fast enough, and don't think, it seems to make sense. But, my friends, it makes no sense. You cannot do both, and no nation in all the history of the world ever succeeded in doing it.

(D3) For twenty-five years Mussolini outlawed Communism, and they grew and flourished underground despite their punishment and their exile and their shooting. As a result, four weeks ago, the Communists and their allies polled more than 30 per cent of the vote in the recent Italian election.

(D4) I spent eleven years of my life as a prosecutor in New York. That was in the days when they said nobody could clean up the organized underworld. They said we had to use the methods of dictators – we have to go out and string them up. I've had judges and people in high places tell me that. But a group of young men took it in, and week after week, month after month, year after year, they worked and they delivered the City of New York from the control of organized crime, and they did it by constitutional means and under the Bill of Rights.

Questions

1. S1 and D4 are lengthy references to self. What qualities of *ethos* are called up by each?
2. What might be the consequences of the association of Henry Wallace and Governor Dewey in S3? How might the processes of Receiving and Focusing be stimulated by this statement?
3. Consider the same questions for the association of "outlaw the Communist party" and "preserve our liberties" in D2.
4. Compare S2 and D1 as differing uses of argument and evidence based upon testimony. In what ways might each be effective?
5. Can you diagram the argument of S4 according to the Toulmin system presented in Chapter 2? What is the unstated conclusion? What other elements of Toulmin's scheme are unstated? Could Stassen expect his audience to *complete* this inference?
6. Suppose that D3 was an influential statement. Explain its possible effectiveness in terms of belief and affect changes which modify an object of judgment. What is the object of judgment? How might the processes of Receiving, Focusing, Associating, and Resolving effect modification of the object of judgment?

RECOMMENDED READINGS

List A

For additional references on persuasion, it is recommended that the works in this list be read first. They are all basic, general, and central to our topic.

ARISTOTLE, *The Rhetoric*, trans. W. R. Roberts (New York: Modern Library, Inc., 1954). Aristotle on influential discourse. The more interested reader will want to supplement this source with other materials by and about Aristotle.

[CICERO], *Ad Herennium*, trans. H. Caplan (London: William Heinemann, Ltd., 1954). The Greek art in Roman dress. Contains in outline form the full scope of classical rhetoric. This systematic, technical manual exerted influence for a thousand years.

CLARK, DONALD L., *Rhetoric in Greco-Roman Education* (New York: Columbia University Press, 1957). An account of rhetorical training in Greece and Rome. Presents an overview of principles, as well as a description of the procedures for using models and practice exercises. Chapter 4, "The Precepts of Rhetoric," is most helpful.

COHEN, ARTHUR R., *Attitude Change and Social Influence* (New York: Basic Books, Inc., 1964). A synthesis of psychological findings on attitude change. The chief advantages of this book are its recency and its summary of work done in psychology. It is limited by the view that serious concern about persuasive discourse started in the 1920's.

EISENSON, JON, J. JEFFERY AUER, and JOHN V. IRWIN, *Psychology of Communication* (New York: Appleton-Century-Crofts, Inc., 1963). Considers the nature, origin, purposes, and psychological principles of oral communication and summarizes much of the research on persuasive speech in various settings. The breadth of treatment is at once the strength and the weakness of this book.

THONSSEN, LESTER, and A. CRAIG BAIRD, *Speech Criticism: The Development of Standards for Rhetorical Appraisal* (New York: Ronald Press Company, 1948). A survey of the development of rhetorical theory and the practice of speech criticism. Intensive treatment of analytical tools and procedures. Somewhat dated approach is compensated for by historical overview.

List B

The works on this second-level list are recommended for the reader who wishes now to delve more deeply into specific concerns and approaches to persuasion.

BERLO, DAVID K., *The Process of Communication: An Introduction to Theory and Practice* (New York: Holt, Rinehart & Winston, Inc., 1960). A general and basic account of the total communicative process. Stresses the role of learning, language, and interaction between communicators in the total process.

BREMBECK, WINSTON L., and WILLIAM S. HOWELL, *Persuasion: A Means of Social Control* (Englewood Cliffs, N.J.: Prentice-Hall, Inc., 1952). A widely used college text for persuasive speaking. Defines persuasion as "the conscious attempt to modify thought and action by manipulating the motives of men toward predetermined ends." Emphasizes psychological and motivational bases of persuasion.

BROWN, JAMES A. C., *Techniques of Persuasion* (Baltimore: Penguin Books, Inc., 1963). An account of persuasion that is typically English. Eclectic, interesting, broad in scope. Contains much anecdotal material on persuasion in society, politics, advertising, brainwashing, etc.

BROWN, ROGER, *Social Psychology* (New York: Free Press of Glencoe, Inc., 1965). Chapter 11, "The Principle of Consistency in Attitude Change," is most helpful. It compares the Congruity model, the Balance model, and the Dissonance model as explanation of the attitude change process.

FESTINGER, LEON, *A Theory of Cognitive Dissonance* (Evanston, Ill.: Row, Peterson & Company, 1957). The source which lays out Festinger's theory of Cognitive Dissonance. An interested reader might want to follow up with Leon Festinger, *Conflict, Decision, and Dissonance* (Stanford: Stanford University Press, 1964).

HOVLAND, CARL I., IRVING L. JANIS, and HAROLD H. KELLEY, *Communication and Persuasion* (New Haven: Yale University Press, 1953). The initial summary volume in the Yale Studies in Attitude and Communication. It considers the influence of the speaker, variables within the message, and attributes of the audience in the communicative setting. The assumptions and goals of the entire series are presented.

KENNEDY, GEORGE, *The Art of Persuasion in Greece* (Princeton, N. J.: Princeton University Press, 1963). Explores rhetorical theory and practice from the fifth to the first centuries B.C. in Greece. Makes clear the preeminent role of speech in the Greek culture.

ROSENBERG, MILTON J., and others, ed., *Attitude Organization and Change* (New Haven: Yale University Press, 1960). One of the Yale Studies in Attitude and Communication. Emphasizes the cognitive approach and attempts to identify and relate the cognitive, affective, and behavioral components of attitudes.

RUESCH, JURGEN, and GREGORY BATESON, *Communication: The Social Matrix of Psychiatry* (New York: W. W. Norton & Company, Inc., 1951). This work combines the efforts of a psychiatrist and an anthropologist who treat communication as a central aspect of life in the normal and abnormal human condition. The broad cultural concern, as well as the insights gained from the interplay of normal and abnormal, are helpful.

SHERIF, CAROLYN W., MUZAFER SHERIF, and ROGER E. NEBERGALL, *Attitude and Attitude Change: The Social Judgment-Involvement Approach* (Philadelphia: W. B. Saunders Company, 1965). A recent publication which points to weaknesses in cognitive dissonance theory and presents an *approach* to attitude change based on studies of social judgments and the effect of ego-involvement on behavior.

List C

This final list of recommended readings should be approached last. The items here are of interest but tend to be narrower in scope, or more specialized, or more complex, or more peripheral.

ASCH, S. E. "The Doctrine of Suggestion, Prestige, and Imitation in Social Psychology," *Psychological Review*, LV (1948), 250–276. An important article by Asch which points to the distinction, important in this volume, between "changes in the judgment of an object" and "changes in the object of judgment."

BERELSON, BERNARD, and GARY A. STEINER, *Human Behavior: An Inventory of Scientific Findings* (New York: Harcourt, Brace & World, Inc., 1964). A significant recent contribution. The authors attempt an inventory and a summary of behavioral science research. Most important for one interested in persuasion are the chapters on the basic psychological processes, "Perceiving," "Learning and Thinking," and "Motivation," as well as those chapters on "Face-to-Face Relations in Small Groups," "Mass Communication," and "Opinions, Attitudes, and Beliefs."

BRUNER, JEROME S., JACQUELINE J. GOODNOW, and GEORGE A. AUSTIN, *A Study of Thinking* (New York: John Wiley & Sons, Inc., 1956). This work summarizes some of the work of a Harvard group studying cognition. It is most helpful in discussing how and why man categorizes and in outlining patterns or strategies for human problem solving.

FISHBEIN, MARTIN, and BERTRAM H. RAVEN, "The AB Scales: An Operational Definition of Belief and Attitude," *Human Relations*, XV (February 1962), 35–44. This article presents the development and validating of a measuring instrument to top personal belief and affect structures. The AB scales are presented, a case is made for their use, and evidence of reliability and validity is presented.

HOVLAND, CARL I., and others, ed., *The Order of Presentation in Persuasion* (New Haven: Yale University Press, 1957). One of the Yale Studies in Attitude and Communication. Considers the primary-recency issue and the effects of order of materials within a communication.

JANIS, IRVING L., and CARL I. HOVLAND, ed., *Personality and Persuasibility* (New Haven: Yale University Press, 1959). One of the Yale Studies. Considers general personality and sex differences in persuasion and devotes some attention to persuasibility in children.

KATZ, DANIEL, ed., "Attitude Change," *The Public Opinion Quarterly*, XXIV, No. 2 (Summer 1960). A special issue of *The Public Opinion Quarterly* devoted to "Attitude Change." Contains, among other good essays, Katz' "The Functional Approach to the Study of Attitudes" and Zajonc's "Balance, Congruity, and Dissonance."

Maslow, A. H., *Motivation and Personality* (New York: Harper & Brothers, 1954). Presents Maslow's general theory of human motivation. Chapter 5 is most important. It contains an outline of five levels of need and the hierarchy of basic needs.

Osgood, Charles E., George J. Suci, and Percy H. Tannenbaum, *The Measurement of Meaning* (Urbana: University of Illinois Press, 1957). Describes a technique for, and the results of, an attempt to measure language meaning. The concept of semantic space is developed and the dimensions of semantic space are presented. Chapter 5, "Attitude Measurement and the Principle of Congruity," is particularly helpful.

Sherif, Muzafer, and Carl I. Hovland, *Social Judgment* (New Haven: Yale University Press, 1961). Presents early work on the relation of the social judgment studies to attitude change. May be read as background to Sherif, Sherif, and Nebergall reference cited above.

Spranger, Eduard, *Types of Men*, trans. by P. Prigors from 5th German edition (Haale [Saale]: M. Niemeyer, 1928). The work which presents this German scholar's views of the pervasive value patterns held by men.

Toulmin, Stephen, *The Uses of Argument* (Cambridge: Cambridge University Press, 1958). An attempt to make sense of logic and argument in realistic social settings. The analytic pattern laid out in Chapter 3, "The Layout of Arguments," is helpful, but the remainder of the book gives substance to the argument for Toulmin's suggested pattern.

Weinberg, Harry L., *Levels of Knowing and Existence* (New York: Harper & Brothers, 1959). A book on the role of language and reasoning from the view of general semantics. Helpful for understanding the arbitrary nature of our language and the manner in which our language constrains us at the same time that it frees us.

INDEX

Abstracting, 33–34
Acceptance, 21. *See also* Persuasive influence.
Active participation. *See* Self persuasion.
Adams, John Quincy, 1
Adaptation, 31–32
Affects, 23–24, 40–42, 57–59, 103, 109. *See also* Persuasive influence.
Allport, Gordon, 45
Aristotle, 1, 8–12, 16–17, 33, 37, 74
Asch, Solomon E., 28, 58
Associating, 69–76, 77–79, 82, 101, 103, 109
Association, 20, 23, 36, 107. *See also* Associating.
Attention, 18–19, 21. *See also* Focusing.
Attitude, 23–24, 26–27, 40–42, 57–59. *See also* Affects, Persuasive influence.
Attitude change. *See* Persuasive influence.
Audience analysis-adaptation, 7, 10–11, 29, 49–52. *See also* Feedback, Speaker-listener interaction.
Augustine, St., 1
Austin, George A., 34, 40
Austin, Gilbert, 16
Authority, 19. *See also* Ethos.

Bacon, Francis, 1, 98–101
Beecher, Henry Ward, 50
Beliefs, 23–24, 40–42, 57–59, 103, 109. *See also* Persuasive influence.
Berelson, Bernard, 56
Boas, Franz, 34
Boomerang effect, 81–82
Brainwashing, 2, 56
Brembeck, Winston, 20
Brigance, William N., 19–20
Brown, Roger, 22
Bruner, Jerome S., 34, 40
Bulwer, John, 16
Burke, Kenneth, 27, 72

Categories, 32–34, 101. *See also* Persuasive influence.
Churchill, Winston, 56–57, 64–65, 91–92
Cicero, 1, 12–13, 15, 74–75
Clark, Donald L., 15
Communication, 2, 90
Completing, 62–64, 77–79, 103. *See also* Receiving.
Comprehension, 21
Compton, Arthur, 30
Concrete, 18
Congruity principle, 22–23
Consistency theories, 22–23, 69–70
Corax, 5
Credibility. *See* Ethos.

Deduction, 11–12
Delivery, 15–16, 18
Demosthenes, 15
Derivations, 7
Dewey, John, 86
Dewey, Thomas E., 11, 107–109
Disposition, 14, 18, 65, 101–102, 106

Edwards, Allen L., 62
Eisenhower, Dwight D., 23, 84
Ego-involvement, 24–26, 63–64
Elocution, 14–15, 102–106
Emotional appeal, 10–11, 37–39, 91–92
Emphasis. *See* Focusing.
Enthymeme, 11–12, 37
Ethics of persuasion, 80–81, 87–95
Ethos, 10, 83–84, 106–107, 109
Evidence. *See* Toulmin model.
Example, 11
Expert testimony, 71, 109. *See also* Ethos.

Fallacy of the Undistributed Middle, 70
Familiar, 18
Feedback, 7, 50, 85
Feelings. *See* Affects.

Feral child, 80
Festinger, Leon, 69
Filtering, 61–62, 77–79, 102. *See also* Receiving.
Fishbein, Martin, 23, 40
Fishbein attitude model, 23–24
Focusing, 65–69, 77–79, 82, 101, 106, 109
Functional autonomy of motives, 45

Geiger counter, 30
Generalizing, 33–34, 63. *See also* Associating.
Gesture, 2. *See also* Delivery.
Gettysburg Address, 78–79, 96–98
Gibbons, Thomas, 14
Goodnow, Jacqueline J., 34, 40
Gorgias, 5

Habit, 45–46
Hamilton, Alexander, 56
Hebb, D. O., 39
Heider, Fritz, 69
Heisenberg principle, 30
Henry, Patrick, 66
Heraclitus, 30
Hippias, 5
Hitler, Adolf, 1, 7–8, 56–57, 92
Hostile audience, 54
Hovland, Carl I., 21, 22, 53, 63, 65
Howell, William, 20
Humor, 67
Hunt, Everett L., 6

Identification, 27, 72, 103, 107. *See also* Associating.
"Idols of the Mind," 98–101
Incongruity, 66, 82
Induction, 11
Inference. *See* Reasoning, Toulmin model.
Inflection, 2, 54. *See also* Delivery.
Ingersoll, Robert G., 67
Intention, 1, 87, 106
Internalization. *See* Self persuasion.
Invention, 13–14, 18, 107–109

James, William, 18, 30, 91, 94
Janis, Irving L., 21, 22, 65
Jargon, 73
Jefferson, Thomas, 58

Katz, Daniel, 26–27
Katz, Elihu, 83

Kelley, Harold H., 21, 65
Kennedy, George, 4
King, Martin Luther, Jr., 56, 101–102

Language, 34–35, 85, 101, 104
Laplace, Pierre Simon de, 29
Learning, 31–32, 76–77. *See also* Resolving.
Lenin, V., 58
Lincoln, Abraham, 78, 96–98, 103–106
Lines of argument. *See* Topics.
Logical appeal, 8, 11–12, 37–39, 91–92. *See also* Reasoning.

Machiavelli, Niccolò, 1, 7
Maslow, A. H., 44, 77; motivational theory, 44
Mead, George Herbert, 81
Meaning, 35, 54, 103. *See also* Persuasive influence.
Memory, 16–17
Mencken, H. L., 91
Metaphor, 66
Modes of persuasion, 9–10, 103, 107
Morley, John, 90–91
Motivation, 20, 43–45, 69–70, 77
Munn, Norman, 35
Mussolini, Benito, 7

Newcomb, Theodore M., 69
Novelty, 18

Object of judgment. *See* Persuasive influence.
Osgood, Charles E., 22, 69

Pareto, Vilfredo, 1, 7
Pellegrini, Angelo M., 8
Perelman, Chaïm, 28
Persuadee, 49–52
Persuader, 49–52
Persuasive influence, description of, 41–42, 55–59, 81–86; explanations of, 17–27, 60–79, 109
Persuasive speaking, consequences of, 81–86; defined, 1–3, 11; end of, *see* Persuasive influence; influence, *see* Persuasive influence; modern approaches, 17–27, 103; occasion, 49–55. *See also* Rhetoric.